# Kitchen Table Stories

A Story Circle Network Anthology of
Stories and Recipes

Edited by M. Jane Ross

**Cover Design and Illustration: Katherine Misegades**
**Editing, Layout, & Coordination: M. Jane Ross**
**Project Support: Peggy Moody**
**Text Illustrations: Susan Gaber, courtesy of Dover Publications Inc.**


Trade edition, 2007
Printed in the United States of America



Published by Story Circle Network
P.O. Box 500127
Austin, TX 78750-0127, U.S.A.
**www.storycircle.org**

The Story Circle Network is dedicated to helping women share the stories of their lives and to raising public awareness of the importance of women's personal histories. We carry out our mission through publications, a website, classes, workshops, writing and reading circles, and woman-focused programs. Our activities empower women to tell their stories, discover their identities through their stories, and choose to be the authors of their own lives.

ISBN 978-0-9795329-3-1 (Trade Edition)

# Contents

# *Lifting the Lid*

**Lavon Urbonas**

I almost tossed it.
Who needs an old aluminum lid,
timeworn and dented?
I didn't. But it belonged to Mom.

Concentric sections rising to a dome,
looking like a helmet for
Don Quixote,
it shielded her from splatters.

Dad replaced the wooden knob
when the original,
worn and brittle,
loosened and came off in her hand.

A spattered testament
to decades of food from scratch,
it's forever freckled
from bits of vittles she deftly prepared.

It conjures up chicken fried in Crisco,
crisp and tender; chili; ham and limas;
steamy aromas
rising as she lifted the lid.

Imperfect, still it perfectly fits
my ten-inch skillet.
Toss it?
Never. It belongs to me.

*Honorable mention in the California State Poetry Society 2006 annual contest. Read Lavon Urbonas' biography on page 109.*

# Foreword

The idea for a cookbook combining stories and recipes from Story Circle Network members was planted two years back by Story Circle Network's Board members, many of them enthusiastic cooks, all of them enthusiastic storytellers and writers. For those who don't already know, Story Circle Network (SCN) is the ground-breaking non-profit organization that works in many ways to encourage women to write about their lives. Founded in 1997 by best-selling mystery writer Susan Wittig Albert, the organization has helped over 1600 women throughout the U.S. and worldwide to experience the life-changing benefits of telling and sharing our own life stories. As SCN's tenth anniversary approached in 2007, the time seemed right to make our cookbook idea happen. The book you now hold in your hands, *Kitchen Table Stories*, is the result, bringing together the food stories and related recipes from over 60 SCN members.

*Kitchen Table Stories* is part of the venerable American tradition of community cookbooks, those eclectic and quirky compilations of recipes put together by so many church committees and non-profits over the past century. *Kitchen Table Stories* is most definitely eclectic. Its recipes include a wide range of dishes, from those that could have come straight out of many a western grandmother's wood-burning stove all the way to decidedly contemporary fare with a nod even to the aromatic cuisine of Asia. *Kitchen Table Stories* is a community effort, assembled by women who aren't renowned chefs or cookery writers. Its appeal for the cookbook lover is that these are the recipes of women a lot like us, each bringing echoes of their heritage and their home place to the table. And *Kitchen Table Stories* has a special quirkiness that sets it apart from other community cookbooks—we've accompanied each recipe with a story, sometimes hilarious, other times touching, always engaging.

Have you ever opened a community cookbook and wondered, Why these particular recipes? Why did this contributor feel such attachment to a simple recipe for a skillet of potatoes and eggs that she wanted to share it with the world? The answer of course is the story behind the recipe and this dish's special meaning for the author. *Kitchen Table Stories* is the recipe collection that gives us these stories. As we read, we are reminded of the special comfort that there is in even the simplest foods, like a plate of potatoes and eggs for breakfast. We can relive the pleasure of a fruit pie that's homemade in the sweet-smelling, flour-dusted kitchen of the childhood we remember or perhaps of the childhood we might have wished for. We can relish the memories that connect a recipe to a beloved family member.

Many of the recipes in *Kitchen Table Stories* and the stories behind them celebrate "slow food," the food of our mothers and grandmothers, made largely from scratch, often with ingredients that came fresh from their own back yards or using the preserves that they had put up for the winter. Some recipes celebrate the creative use of leftovers, a skill our resourceful foremothers often turned into an art. Other recipes are tributes to the ingenuity of busy women living contemporary lifestyles. Our stories tell of celebrations around the dining table; they tell of the tensions that surrounded food and cooking in some of our homes. Always, they are the stories of real women reflecting on what food and cooking has meant to them, in their own well-chosen words.

This is a book that calls for a comfortable reading chair, a cup of something hot to drink, and a favorite sweet treat to nibble on while you sit and savor the stories of this diverse group of women writers and cooks. And it's a book you'll want to take into your kitchen to try out the enticing and varied recipes that come paired with our stories.

Above all, this book is a community effort that celebrates something bigger than each of us individually. It celebrates our stories and the place that food and cooking has in all our lives. I hope it will inspire you to reflect, as you cook, as you gather with friends and family at the table, and as you eat, on the stories behind the foods in your own life. And I hope it will inspire you to write those stories down to share with those who will come after you. We've added a few choice writing prompts to get you started!

*Jane Ross*
Editor, Austin, Texas, 2007

## A Note from SCN's President

Memories and meals make great kitchen table talk. *Kitchen Table Stories* is filled with both—from a young girl's excitement with her first chicken fried steak to the scented memories of a grandmother's chicken and dumplings—recipes to try and stories to cherish. This is more than a cookbook; filled with contributions from members of Story Circle Network from across the country it is a pleasure to read. Don't be at all surprised if it inspires you to write down some long-forgotten kitchen table stories of your own and perhaps to head to the kitchen to cook up your past.

*Patricia Pando*
President, Story Circle Network

This project owes an enormous debt to very many wonderful women. My sincere thanks to all of you:

To Katherine Misegades for her beautiful illustration and design for the book cover;

To Peggy Moody for invaluable administrative help;

To all the volunteer editors who worked with their fellow SCN members and authors during the first phase of the book: Janet Caplan, Melody Gordon, Penny Leisch, Theresa May, Nancy Rigg, Tricia Stephens, Becca Taylor, Beth van Duzer, Judy Whelley, and Linda Wisniewski;

To our eagle-eyed proofreaders, Peggy Grose, Penny Leisch, Danelle Sasser, Sandra Simon, and Bonnie Watkins;

To Judy Abrahamson for shipping assistance;

To everyone who packed books, stuck stamps, or in any way helped during this project;

And of course, to all the authors of the book, without whom we would not be here! (You can read the author biographies alongside each of their stories, poems, and recipes, and you'll find a complete alphabetic index of contributors in the rear of the book.)

To Susan Wittig Albert for having the vision and energy to start Story Circle Network and for the confidence you have placed in me over the past five years;

To Patricia Pando for steering the ship of SCN so deftly through its tenth anniversary year as its President;

To Judith Helburn and Danelle Sasser for your wonderful friendship and moral support;

Last but most definitely not least, my eternal love to Felipe and Sofia and my thanks for helping me stay grounded throughout this project. And my love and thanks to my first cooking teacher, my mother Elisabeth Ross.

*JR*

# *Breakfasts*

# Breakfast Cheesecake

**Mary Jo Doig**

"Momma," my daughter, Polly, calls up the staircase. "Can Sue and I eat the cheesecake in the fridge for breakfast?"

I pause as I rinse my face with cool water. Hmm. I wonder, what kind of nutrition does cheesecake give a seven- and nine-year-old with a full day of school ahead?

"Mom?" she calls, a little louder.

"Wait. I'm thinking," I reply, squeezing moisturizer onto my palm. I gently apply the scented cream as I consider Polly's question. Cream cheese and eggs are good protein. Cheesecake is low in sugar. Hmm, that combination could sustain a whole morning of schoolwork. I walk to the top of the curved wooden staircase in the century-old farmhouse. "Okay, go ahead," I say, smiling at the wide, dark-eyes that look hopefully up at me. I know she and Sue will be thrilled; yet I'm still a little doubtful.

"Yippee! We can have it, Sue!" Polly shouts happily.

Breakfast is, indeed, a delight that morning and cheesecake is the main reason. Then, our morning routines complete, we walk down the hill, get into my car, and drive into town. My daughters hop out to wait with neighbor children until the school bus pulls up. When they step up to the bus, I hold up my left hand in the universal sign-language gesture for "I love you." They smile, returning the gesture. I begin my twenty-mile drive to work.

Cheesecake for breakfast, I ponder, intrigued. Everyone loves cheesecake, after all; the real problem is fat and I don't want my girls to start their day with just a lot of fat. Can I create a cheesecake food that would be soundly nutritional for breakfast? I wonder. The late-winter, quiet, Catskill-mountain miles pass nearly unnoticed as I continue thinking. I can cut down the fat and still keep good protein but I need to add some good carbohydrates.

Say! What about granola? I make my own granola once a week, and I begin to quickly review the wholesome ingredients: old-fashioned oats, sesame seeds, sunflower seeds, slivered almonds, and wheat germ, mixed lightly with a little honey and oil, then baked until golden.

Yes! My heart excitedly beats a little faster. I could sprinkle granola on top of the cheesecake mixture and bake it. Or I could make the granola into a crust and bake the cheesecake in it.

Indeed, this idea seems to be coming together, but still I feel I'm not quite there yet. I consider the food pyramid: oh—of course—they will need some fruit!

Let's see: cheesecake and strawberries, cheesecake and blueberries, cheesecake and peaches, cheesecake and—well, any fruit, when you come to think about it. Nothing's in season now. Then I remember the dozens of my canned Georgia peaches placed on the sagging wooden shelves in the ancient cellar where the annual harvest of canned vegetables, fruits, and even meat have resided for decades.

I soon try out a newly devised recipe. As my daughters

---

**Mary Jo Doig** lives in Raphine, Virginia, and has been a member of SCN since 2001, when she joined SCN's writing eCircle 2. She has facilitated ecircle 7 since 2003, and been True Words editor for the *Story Circle Journal* since 2004. A full-time human services professional, she also enjoys freelance opportunities. Reading, writing, editing, cooking, quilting, and knitting are her loves—that is, right after her three great, grown children: Chip, Polly, and Susan.

watch—and help—with great interest, I swirl ingredients in the blender then pour them into four big brown, earthenware bowls. We arrange sliced peaches on top and then liberally sprinkle granola.

And soon the taste test. Ahh, we love it!

The next weekend I spray the bowls, then press granola around the entire surface, place sliced peach slices on the granola "crust," then pour in the cheesecake mixture and bake. We love that variation, too!

We decide it really doesn't matter if the granola or peaches are on the top or the bottom. The girls are delighted to eat cheesecake for breakfast and I'm happy, too, because we are all getting a great start to our day.

A few months later our daily newspaper advertises their annual cooking contest. Shy though I am, I nevertheless send in my entry and am so pleased when my recipe is chosen as a finalist.

On bake-off day Polly comes with me. As we unpack supplies, the bowls I pre-prepared so that they can be tasted chilled, fall onto the pavement and shatter. Polly, who has been unloading them, looks up at me with huge tears in her eyes.

"It's okay, Polly. You are more precious than any bowl of breakfast cheesecake," I reassure her, then hug her.

She smiles, wiping away tears with her small bent forefinger, as I tell her the one remaining bowl will surely be enough.

At day's end my recipe places third of twelve, with a lovely set of Noritake china for eight as my gift. Today, nearly thirty years later, its value has increased amazingly but, in my heart, the true gift of that day is the nurturing moment following broken earthenware between my daughter and me.

### Ingredients

- 1 pint low-fat (2%) cottage cheese
- 2 eggs
- ½ cup sugar
- ½ cup milk
- 2 tablespoons lemon juice
- 1 teaspoon vanilla
- 4 pieces of fruit (or a 29-ounce can of any desired fruit)
- Granola (optional)

### Preparation

Put all ingredients except the fruit and granola into a blender or food processor and swirl until thick and smooth. Lightly spray 4 ovenproof cereal bowls or an 8x8-inch baking dish with cooking spray.

Using 4 sliced peaches or a can of drained, sliced peaches (or any desired fruit), divide fruit evenly over the bottom of the bowls or dish. Pour the cheesecake mixture over the fruit. If desired, sprinkle about 2 tablespoons of granola on top. Bake at 350°F. for 25–30 minutes or until set and golden.

Serves 4.

### Tips and Notes

You can use a sugar substitute such as Splenda in place of the sugar, if desired.

Breakfast Cheesecake can be enjoyed either at room temperature or chilled overnight.

# *Potato Pan Eggs*

**Cindy Bellinger**

Eggs. My mother grew up on a chicken ranch during the Depression and never forgot eggs were cheap and easy. "You better eat them," she'd glare, slapping plates of scrambled, fried or poached, hard or soft-boiled eggs before us each morning. Eggs, however they're cooked, blur through tears. I know this. And know that flavor vanishes with the reprimand, "Just be lucky you have something to eat!"

But the years passed and that luck shifted. I don't have to eat eggs anymore. Except one kind: a stir-fry of sorts with potatoes. Yum. Whenever my mother fixed these, breakfast couldn't come soon enough.

"It's how Grandpa made them for Mama," she said when I told her once how good they were.

Crunchy with soft spots and a little burned, the whole concoction makes a feast every time. Odd that through at least four generations, this family specialty never had a name. Then early one morning, I softly asked: "Can we have those 'potato pan eggs' tomorrow?" And the name stuck—just the way the eggs did, just for a few seconds, on the bottom of the pan.

When my mother arrived for a visit many years ago, I called out one morning: "Want some Potato Pan Eggs?"

"Well," she huffed, "do you know how to fix them?"

She meant did I have the potatoes ready. And that's the key—use cold, cooked potatoes. Whenever preparing baked or boiled potatoes, I always toss in a few more of the nodules for the following morning.

As a kid, I discovered Potato Pan Eggs were delicious with lots of salt.

"Don't use so much salt. Grandpa died of a stroke, you know," she warned as we ate our favorite breakfast out on the patio. Yes, I now use fake salt—except when eating Potato Pan Eggs. After all, what's life without a few pleasures?

---

**Cindy Bellinger,** a journalist for thirty years, recently published *Journaling for Women: Write, Doodle, Scribble! and Meet Yourself Up Close*. She is also featured in *What Wildness Is This*. She makes her living by writing and cooks up a storm in the mountains of northern New Mexico.

## Ingredients

Potatoes, one per person, boiled and cooled
Butter
Eggs, one per person
Salt and pepper to taste

## Preparation

Cut cold, cooked potatoes into bite-size chunks and fry them in butter. Make sure they brown and that some of the edges burn. Turn the heat up higher. Make those potatoes sizzle! Now crack the eggs on the edge of the skillet; dump them onto the potatoes. Stir quickly, letting some of the eggs stick. Season. Done!

## Tips and Notes

There *are* rules for making Potato Pan Eggs:

- Use cold, cooked potatoes;
- Don't measure anything;
- Sprinkle liberally with salt—even if your mother is watching.

# *Christmas Day Sausage Bread*

**Judy Whelley**

Our Christmas Day Open House began the year my husband and I created our own Christmas celebration for our son. Prior to this, we usually traveled to one of the grandparents' houses for the big day. We decided to save the out-of-town family travel for December twenty-sixth. With no immediate family in the area and still craving the joy of a full house on Christmas, we extended an invitation to all our local friends—just come, anytime! And so a new tradition began.

I wanted to serve food that would be appropriate no matter the time of day, was served hot, and was easy to prepare yet delicious. I remembered a sausage bread that I enjoyed at a friend's house some years before. The recipe was found and duly prepared. That sausage bread was devoured by all with rave reviews. As the years went by, it became a tradition. I now bake about a dozen loaves throughout the day. The first guests usually arrive around noon and the last leave around ten. Friends plan their visits to overlap with one another. It has become a day rich with love, laughter, and sharing.

When my husband and I separated, the first question after the initial shock was, "What about your Christmas Open House and the *sausage bread*?" I assured one and all that the tradition would continue. The first year was hard. It is difficult to see a long marriage end, and friendships needed to be adjusted a bit. But sausage bread and love ruled the day. The tradition was strengthened and continues to the present.

Christmas Day is the only time I make this bread. I've shared the recipe freely but my friends claim it never tastes as good as it does when they have it at my home. I tell them the secret ingredient is the love I have for them combined with the magic of Christmas and shared laughter.

---

Some of **Judy Whelley's** favorite memories are around the preparation and sharing of food. She's recently retired after a thirty-three-year career in education, teaching students from preschool through the doctoral level. She's an adventurous cook, eager to attempt and adapt new recipes. Judy joined the Internet Chapter of the Story Circle Network in 2006. She lives in Dayton, Ohio, with her son Brendan and two Yorkies.

# *Christmas Day Sausage Bread*

## Ingredients

- ½ pound grated Cheddar or Colby cheese
- 1 teaspoon garlic salt
- 1 teaspoon parsley
- 3 eggs (save ½ of one egg to brush on top)
- ¼ pound grated Swiss cheese
- 2 tablespoons grated Parmesan cheese
- 2 packages crescent rolls
- 1–2 pounds bulk sausage (mix regular and hot, if desired)

## Preparation

Preheat the oven to 350°F.

Combine the first 6 ingredients.

Pinch the crescent rolls together to make 2 large rectangles. Sprinkle (or mash!) sausage over each rectangle. Then spread the egg/cheese mixture over each and pat down. Roll each rectangle like a jelly roll, starting at one of the long edges. Place each roll, seam side down, in a glass baking dish. Tuck the ends and brush with the remaining egg.

Bake 35–45 minutes at 350°F. Allow to cool before serving.

Makes 2 large or 4 small loaves.

## Tips and Notes

Loaves can be frozen after baking. Allow to cool first.

# *Irish Griddle Scones*

**Janice Kvale**

"I've made scones!"

These words greeted my mother, father, and me as we arrived after a long day's drive to Auntie's house. Indeed, the smell of fresh scones, mixed with the odor of the kerosene lamps that lit the kitchen, titillated our senses. My mother exulted great pleasure over this special treat for dinner. Our arrival created great excitement for hosts and visitors alike. That night, I fell asleep listening to my mother and her sister talk late into the night.

Scones (correctly pronounced *skawns* among Scots–Irish descendants) were a cultural icon for our family. No longer a daily necessity, this bread of the commonplace became a symbol of remembrance. Remembrance of what, I didn't always appreciate.

As I grew older and more thoughtful, I imagined my great-grandmother, the only grandmother who survived beyond my infancy, making this bread daily to feed her impoverished family. Likewise, her mother before her would have made them in Ireland on an iron griddle because they had no oven.

Scones became a traditional breakfast on Christmas morning for our family. As long as she lived, Auntie made the scones for both families weeks before Christmas and put them in the freezer. Christmas Eve, they were removed from the freezer to thaw. On Christmas morning, they were reheated in bacon fat on the griddle and served with bacon, fried eggs, and strawberry jam. After Auntie died, my mother took over making scones for the family for Christmas morning, but she followed Auntie in death a short three years later.

My daughters took up the tradition and I thought I had dodged the task. But they married and moved in different directions across the country. To keep the tradition alive, I had to learn to make scones. I hunted for the recipe in the inherited recipe boxes from my mother and aunt. Not there. Then I looked in my own box of collected recipes. There it was in my sixteen-year-old hand writing. Then I remembered, many years before, I had asked Auntie for the recipe for scones.

"I never measure, so I don't know," she had replied. But, together we made scones. She used handfuls of flour, scoops of lard, and poured small amounts of salt and baking powder into her hand. We measured and estimated and came up with a recipe. But I never had to make them, relying on others through the years. Finally, it was my turn.

I learned that despite a recipe, it was a skill requiring experience. Sometimes the dough felt just right and I knew I had a good outcome. Other times, the amount of lard wasn't right for the dryness of the flour and adjustments were made. Regardless of how the scones turned out, Christmas morning would be incomplete without bacon, eggs, scones, and strawberry jam.

---

As a person who enjoys creative writing and almost became a journalist, **Jan Kvale** was delighted when she somehow stumbled across Story Circle Network. She's a bit of a vagabond with a home in Austin, Texas, and a cabin in northern Minnesota. Jan is fortunate enough to have traveled and worked internationally and is writing a memoir of the year she and her husband were Fulbright Senior Scholars in India.

# Irish Griddle Scones

### Ingredients

| | |
|---|---|
| 4 | cups flour |
| 1 | teaspoon salt |
| 1 | tablespoon sugar |
| 1 | teaspoon baking soda |
| 3 | teaspoons baking powder |
| 5 | tablespoons lard |
| 1½ | cups buttermilk or sour milk |

### Preparation

Blend dry ingredients. Work lard into dry ingredients until the consistency of coarse meal. Add the buttermilk or sour milk and mix gently, just until a soft dough forms and all dry ingredients are moist. Divide dough in half, place onto a floured surface, and knead each half a few times.

In turn, pat each half until it forms a round (or square or rectangle) about ½ inch thick. Then cut into biscuit-size portions—squares or wedges. (Over the years, I have come to prefer pie shaped wedges, though my aunt and mother made squares. The reason becomes obvious with the baking of the scones.)

Bake the scones on a dry griddle over low to moderate heat (about 300°F. on an electric griddle) until brown on one side. Turn them over and bake until brown on the other side. Then each cut edge must also be baked until brown (and those triangular wedges only have 3 sides instead of 4 to turn and cook). This ensures the scones are thoroughly baked through.

Makes 2-dozen scones.

### Tips and Notes

They can be eaten fresh and hot with butter and jam. Saved for Christmas morning or a special breakfast, they are fried on the griddle in the fat from bacon, imparting additional flavor. My mother insisted that strawberry jam on the scones complemented the flavor of the bacon and fried eggs. I figure all that fat ingested one day out of the year honors my Irish forbears who, unlike me, probably needed all the fat they could get.

# *Mothers and Muffins*

**Janice Kvale**

Though I grew up in a rural area, I had grown used to the anonymity of living in a city. Moving back to a small rural town was culture shock. It seemed like everyone knew where you went, when you went, and if you didn't go, why. One of the things that puzzled me most was the "coffee klatches" that, as the new doctor's wife, I was expected to attend. Most of the women who were included were stay-at-home mothers, as I too now was to our two little girls.

The self-appointed hostess would call everyone with an invitation for "coffee," date and hour specified. The invitees would arrive at the specified time, dressed in casual but better-than-around-the-house clothing, offspring in tow. The uncluttered home looked as though Merry Maids had just left. One or more home-baked goodies would be served in addition to coffee. The hostess strived to serve something no one else had served before, and the recipe was invariably requested. Conversation centered on home decoration, sewing or craft projects, church activities (there were only Protestant churches in this homogeneous town of 900 souls), husbands, and children. Everyone's children were admired and cooed over in turn.

Secretly, I felt superior to my contemporaries and this charade of one-up-womanship. The ritual seemed purposeless and designed to establish a hierarchy of women. Those mothers who found it necessary or chose to be employed were rarely included. A few who could have been included stayed aloof from this social life. I admired them.

Knowing that my turn would be coming, I observed carefully how to dress, how to behave, and what to serve. My gravest concern was having my house in order. I admit to being only a so-so housekeeper, and with two preschoolers, clutter (not to mention dust bunnies) was the standard condition of my home. One day I was casually visiting a friend who was renowned for her coffee party productions. She had four children, yet her home was never cluttered.

"How do you always have your home so neat?" I risked asking.

She gave me a conspiratorial glance.

"I have a little trick. When I have company coming over, I take a cake pan, fill it with the clutter that is about and stick it in the oven."

Armed with what seemed a sure solution to entertaining in a neat-as-a-pin house, I planned my coffee party. I enjoyed the culinary aspects of homemaking, so producing a home-baked product wasn't as intimidating as having an acceptably clean house. I set the date, invited the guests, and shamelessly planned to serve Six-Weeks Muffins, which I was sure would be an impressive new addition to the cuisine of the town.

There was no sense in cleaning the house too far ahead of the hour; it would just descend into chaos again before the party, which I wisely planned for the afternoon. Surveying my domain the morning of my coffee gathering, I decided the cake pan idea might not be ambitious enough for what I saw. I grabbed a clothes basket and started picking up. When the basket was full, there was still plenty of clutter. With a sigh, I emptied the basket, putting each thing in an appropriate, hidden place. I filled the basket again, with the same outcome. With less patience, I repeated the emptying. Then I filled the basket again for the last time, shoved it in a closet, and slammed the door shut. I had just enough time to bake the muffins I had planned. A friend had shared a recipe with me for Six-Weeks Muffins, probably obtained off a cereal box somewhere, and I altered it to suit my organic and natural product inclinations.

At the coffee party, my Six-Weeks Muffins recipe was requested multiple times. I knew each woman would in turn make the recipe for someone else, who would be pleased with a new recipe to try. I had put a surprise, a date, in the middle of each muffin. They were a hit. We talked about our kids, the latest home extension classes (a group I had also joined), and our husbands, who were mostly preoccupied in their own worlds. I had become one of them.

Over time my interpretation of the coffee party phenomenon changed. Women confined primarily at home with young children crave adult conversation. Many are trapped in the American experience of men married to their jobs and women completely fixated on their offspring. Getting together served the purpose of providing adult companionship, an exchange of mutually interesting information, an opportunity for their children to play with others, and, probably most important, a stress reliever. I didn't totally buy into my need for this diversion, though in retrospect I found it as much a life raft as the other women did. But I respected it for what, at that time, I understood it to mean to others.

*See Janice Kvale's biography on page 8.*

# Jan's Six-Weeks Muffins

### Ingredients

- 1 quart buttermilk
- 1⅓ cups oil
- 2 cups water
- 2 cups honey
- 4 eggs, beaten
- 6 cups miller's bran (or bran cereal)
- 5 cups whole wheat flour
- 5 teaspoons baking soda
- 2 teaspoons salt
- Fruit, such as raisins, cranberries, blueberries, or chopped dates

### Preparation

Preheat the oven to 400°F. In a very large bowl, combine the wet ingredients and mix well. Add the dry ingredients and mix well. When you are ready to bake a batch of muffins, add fruit to the batter, using ¼ cup of fruit per cup of muffin batter. Fill greased muffin tins or paper muffin cups about ⅔ full, and bake at 400°F. for 20 minutes.

Makes 6-dozen muffins.

### Tips and Notes

For the buttermilk, you may substitute 4 cups of water mixed with 1½ cups dry buttermilk.

Add chopped walnuts or pecans to the batter before baking, or sprinkle on top for a toasted nut flavor.

Lightly coat paper muffin cups with baking spray to prevent sticking.

Prepared batter, minus the fruit, can be kept in the refrigerator and baked up in small batches quickly and easily.

# *Sunday Mornings—Prishtina to Austin*

**Aferdita Dauti-Heilman**

Sunday morning in Austin, Texas, and Spring Break has officially started. We are almost ready for our annual trip to the beach. I smell enticing aromas of the coffee, toast, bacon, and eggs that my darling husband Stephen, whom I lovingly call Stefan, makes almost every Sunday morning. I know how lucky I am to be pampered by my doting husband.

Our life together started in early spring of 1992. We met in my hometown Prishtina, capitol of Kosova, an autonomic region in then-Yugoslavia. As a medical doctor he came to Kosova on a volunteer mission to vaccinate children with the humanitarian agency, Doctors of the World. As our eyes met, we both knew that this was *it*.

I remember when we shared our first meal together—it was one Sunday morning in May. Stefan and I just met one week earlier. I didn't feel good that day and decided instead to invite him over for breakfast after he had called and asked me to go out.

But what was I going to make? I opened the fridge and didn't see much. I felt that I rushed by inviting him over—perhaps I should have just gone out with him.

Times were quite tough in every respect since the war was already going strong in most of Bosnia, which like Kosova was also part of Yugoslavia. A shortage of food was ever-present, as it was for many other supplies for normal life. A dozen eggs would last a week for my parents and me. A liter of milk was expensive, as were many other items. Looking into my fridge I was feeling very sad, but knowing that I would soon talk to Stefan made me feel better. I knew that I would have the chance to hear more about someone else's life from another life's perspective.

Then I heard the doorbell. A big, open smile and velvety baby-blue eyes greeted me. Deep inside, I felt that I had known him forever. I didn't stress about what I was going to make. He took the chair by the kitchen window with the view from the fifth-floor apartment that we lived in. We heard nine bells, which greet the neighborhood every Sunday, coming from the tower of the local Catholic church on the south side of Prishtina. The hand-held coffee grinder got planted in his hands as I was getting the ingredients together for breakfast. Milk, eggs, flour, and some oil were soon resting together on the table waiting for me.

Stefan was telling me about his days in Jamaica. Laughing children loved to follow him around after their visit at the local clinic. Then he started telling me about his days in West Africa. His words made me feel that I had been there also.

Oops—water in the coffee pot was just about to boil over. As I poured freshly ground coffee in the pot, we

*Continues on page 14*

---

**Dita Dauti-Heilman** was born in the '60s in Kosova, autonomic region in former Yugoslavia. She was raised under a different political system, saw it crumble, and learned the necessity of getting the energy to "pick up and make things work!" Dita is a member of the Wordweavers writing group and SCN since early 2003. By writing about places, people, and times from her two worlds, she brings them closer to her heart, her family, and her readers. She cherishes JFK's words, "Ask not what your country can do for you. Ask what you can do for your country."

# *Dita's Pallaqinkas*

**(French/Austrian Crepes)**

### Ingredients

4 eggs, room temperature
2 cups milk, lukewarm
1 cup sifted white flour
2 tablespoons vegetable oil
(or ½ teaspoon of butter for each *pallaqinka*)
Pinch of salt
Pinch of sugar

### Preparation

Beat the eggs lightly, along with the pinch of salt and sugar, using a wire beater. Add the milk and mix slowly while pouring in the sifted flour. As needed, add more milk so the batter will be smooth and silky but not runny. Add oil and let the batter rest while you read the comics or the Sunday magazine.

Use a nonstick crepe skillet. (You may find them at any good kitchen store.) Over medium heat, pour half a ladle of batter onto the skillet. Turn them as soon as you see that the batter is set and has turned a golden color. With experience, you'll flip the skillet and turn the *pallaqinka* up in the air. After the other side is done, gently place the crepe on a warm flat plate covered with a kitchen towel.

Makes 1 dozen (using a 10-inch pan).

### Tips and Notes

For the first *pallaqinka*, you may use some spray-on oil; the rest should not stick since there is already some oil in the batter.

For the filling you may use any kind of cheese, jam, or honey. They can be sweet or savory, and you may add any filling you like, folding or rolling the filled crepe. My mother told me that I loved them sprinkled with sugar or with rosehip jam.

Oh, don't forget to add 2–3 pinches of love; it helps.

*Continued from page 12*

were already talking about American politics and the upcoming elections. As we were carefully sipping black Balkan coffee from the delicate demitasse cups, we both felt that our conversation was just starting.

By then the smooth and silky batter for the golden *pallaqinkas* was ready and resting for a bit. I started making them by gently pouring a small ladleful of batter and then turning the skillet around. We kept on talking. I kept flipping flying *pallaqinkas*, and soon we were rolling them with some leftover feta cheese and my mother's delicious apricot jam.

After breakfast we decided to go for a walk. We walked up to the station to catch the blue number-four city bus to take us to Germija, the Zilker Park of Prishtina. I heard about the flowers in the Texas Hill Country and the hike and bike trail around Town Lake. On the way back, we were talking about the crazy political situation in Yugoslavia. Suddenly, I wished that I was someplace else since I alone couldn't do much to change the situation. I didn't like the feeling of being helpless in those days.

Many years later, many miles away from the rolling hills of Germija and Kosova, Stefan told me that he knew that if someone can flip that kind of tasty treat for breakfast from the ingredients stored in a half-empty fridge, she would never let him wander hungry and speechless. Love continues to speak its own language of understanding between the two of us.

Let me enjoy my breakfast now. Have I told you that after breakfast we will be leaving for the beach? And, of course, our boys do love their *pallaqinkas* with just plain sugar.

---

## *Food and Love*

**A Writing Prompt**

Many of us have had the experience of falling in love over food. Sometimes the bond didn't last. Sometimes it was the beginning of a long and beautiful relationship.

The times we bond over shared foods stretch far beyond "romantic dinners," as Dita discovered. We can fall in love over a skillet of crepes shared at the kitchen table, over cafeteria food in school, over rations shared in the wilderness, or snacks shared on a street corner.

Think back to the part that food played in some of the falling-in-love experiences from your own life. Note down some of the times, places, and foods you shared. Then choose one of these memories to write a story.

# *Breads*

# *Bread + Jam = Friendship*

**Lee Ambrose**

My childhood hometown in central Pennsylvania was the picture of 1950s Americana. The neighborhood didn't change much. The residents of Reno Street had been there for many years and would likely stay for many more to come.

There was one exception. The home directly across the alley had been sold at a public auction when widower Hesketh moved in with his daughter. The new occupants were quiet and a bit, well,—odd! Or so we thought. Mom was quick to hush us as we discussed this fact at the breakfast table.

"They're not odd. They're Dunkards," she stated matter-of-factly.

"Dunkards?"

We giggled at the sound of the word. The boys began dunking their toast. Mom sighed and shook her head.

Other than knowing that they always had laundry hung on the line to dry before anyone else was even up, we had no clue how they spent their time. Their simple style of dress, complete with white or black bonnets, made them all the more mysterious.

One morning, shortly after the Dunkards moved in, I woke to the smell of freshly baked bread. I silently wondered who it was for this time. Mom always made it for someone else or as a bake sale donation. We rarely enjoyed the crusty treat ourselves. My mouth watered at the thought of savoring a slice of still-warm-from-the-oven bread.

Just then, Mom came in the back door carrying a Mason jar. She had taken a loaf of bread as a welcome-to-the-neighborhood gift.

The Dunkards had given her a jar of homemade jam.

That was one of the only times Mom made bread and didn't give it all away. Every time I smell fresh baked bread, I remember the golden-crusted loaves Mom baked. I also remember the day that the Dunkard ladies sweetened not only our bread but also our lives by sharing a bit of themselves.

---

**Lee Ambrose** works as a travel RN and is currently on assignment in Tennessee. Lee has been a member of Story Circle Network's Internet Chapter for more than six years and loves her participation in its writing eCircles. Words are her passion. When she is not at work, she can be found writing, reading, or doing mixed media art that includes creative journaling.

# *Jean's Streamlined White Bread*

## Ingredients

| | |
|---|---|
| 1 | package active dry yeast |
| 1¼ | cups warm water |
| 2 | tablespoons soft shortening |
| 2 | teaspoons salt |
| 2 | tablespoons sugar |
| 3 | cups flour, sifted |
| | Melted butter |

## Preparation

Dissolve the yeast in warm water in a large bowl. Add the shortening, salt, sugar, and 1½ cups of the flour. Beat the mixture 2 minutes at medium speed with a mixer. Scrape the batter from the sides and bottom of the bowl frequently. Add the remaining 1½ cups of flour and blend the mixture with a spoon until smooth. Scrape the sides of the bowl. Cover the bowl with a cloth, and let the batter rise in a warm place for about 30 minutes.

Then, beat the batter 25 strokes by hand and spread it evenly in a greased loaf pan. Smooth the top of the batter and pat it into shape with floured hands. Let it rise again until the batter reaches 1 inch from the top of the pan (40–60 minutes).

Preheat the oven to 375°F.

Bake 45–50 minutes at 375°F. Remove the bread from the pan, and brush the top with melted butter. Cool before cutting.

Makes 1 loaf.

# Spunky

**Liz Dudley**

"What's a stray dog hair between me and my culinary creations," I asked myself as I puttered around the kitchen on that soft, spring day. Then, as sure as yeast rises, the transient thought gave way to the *sight* of one that I would have to pick out of the onions, carrots, and celery waiting their trip to the chicken stock pot simmering on the stove.

Outside, the clothes waved at the breeze, and inside, the dogs were my company—good company, too—as I chopped and diced, mixed and sliced. I thought for a minute about my life and my career in journalism, and it pleased me that I didn't miss it at all. Life was good.

Barney and Annie were asleep on the wooden floor under the dining room table. Mascot, plunked on his butt in the living room, scratched the wiry salt-and-pepper fur behind his left ear, while Spunky click, click, clicked his toenails from kitchen to sun porch to back door looking for something, anything, to get into, bolt out of, or just generally annoy.

It was the Irish setter in him. The others were so different. Not much ruffled big, red Barney, a brother setter but slower and calmer, or Annie, a curious mix of beagle and fox terrier, or Mascot, an even more curious mix in a slightly bigger package.

No, not even a hair on the cutting board could spoil this day.

When the chicken was picked and the rest of the ingredients added to the soup, I went to the toasty warm sun room to check the progress of the bread dough I'd left to rise. I found an empty bowl, and I knew who was responsible. Of course I did. Come to think of it, he even looked guilty, a smarty-pants-guilty look, but guilty nonetheless. Oh, yes, Spunky, my merry Irish setter.

I yelled. I said words that are bad for little children to hear. I stomped my foot. Look, I enjoy making bread; I find it cathartic to pound dough into tomorrow, but it is some work and takes a bit of time. So I yelled some more at Spunky, whose eyes sparkled with delight as his red-haired tail end wagged hard enough to dislodge a month's worth of dust bunnies. Spunky never got upset. Nothing could get Spunky down as he went about his and everyone else's business. His entire world was a run in the woods after an elusive rabbit he never caught, a bone that came through the drawer at the bank's drive-up window, or a road-kill groundhog. He never believed that out of the entire population of, say, Harrisburg, Pennsylvania, there would be one single person who would not delight in having him plant his two front paws firmly on their chest.

But I got over it. I loved that stupid dog more than what probably would have been the pinnacle loaf of my bread-making career. By the time we went to bed, Spunky was forgiven that for which he had no idea he should be forgiven.

But something happened on the way to morning. A rich smell, a rich yeasty smell, permeated the bedroom. It was

---

**Liz Dudley** is recently retired from a long career as an editor of three weekly newspapers, a job that included covering cops and courts and municipal meetings, as well as taking photographs. Her three children are grown. She and her husband Mike live in Perry County, Pennsylvania, on the top of a hill, with their two Newfys, a Jack Russell terrier, and a multi-mix cat.

coming from the floor and from both ends not of unjustly accused Spunky but...of Mascot, innocent-looking Mascot, who by early morning was down and out and not able to stumble to his feet.

The vet said he was drunk as a skunk, and although I never knew a drunken skunk, I took his word for it. It was the yeast, you know, just like making beer. The only remedy was a stay-over at the veterinarian's so the doctor could monitor him.

That old bread stealer eventually got better. It was a first for our vet, though, and he vowed to submit an account of the mishap to his veterinary journal.

As for Spunky, even though he had been gravely maligned in the drama, he was happy to see Mascot come home. But then, Spunky was happy to watch the grass grow.

# Sally Lunn Bread

### Ingredients

| | |
|---|---|
| 4 | cups all-purpose flour |
| 1 | package active dry yeast |
| 1 | cup milk |
| ½ | cup margarine or butter |
| ⅓ | cup sugar |
| 1 | teaspoon salt |
| 3 | eggs |
| 1 | teaspoon finely shredded lemon peel |

### Preparation

Stir together 2 cups of the flour and the yeast. In a saucepan, heat and stir the milk, margarine or butter, sugar, and salt until the mixture is warm and the margarine almost melts. Add the melted mixture to the flour mixture. Add the eggs. Beat the mixture with a mixer on low speed for 30 seconds, scraping the sides of the bowl constantly. Continue beating the mixture on high speed for 3 minutes. Stir in the remaining flour and the lemon peel.

Cover the bowl and let the dough rise in a warm place until double in size. Lightly grease a 10-inch tube pan or fluted tube pan. Stir the dough down and transfer it to the tube pan. Cover and let it rise again in a warm place until nearly double.

Preheat the oven to 350°F.

Bake at 350°F. for about 40 minutes or until the bread sounds hollow when lightly tapped. Remove the bread from the pan immediately, and serve warm or cool.

Makes 1 loaf.

# The Mandel Bread Pan

**Robin Edgar**

My kids were all in bed, and I was cleaning up the aftermath of macaroni-and-cheese and algebra homework. Something was stuck in the oven drawer, and I could not get it to shut. After a one-sided wrestling match, I finally pulled the whole darn thing out, falling backwards and landing on my bottom. Accompanying this thud were the drums and cymbals of pots and pans crashing to the floor. From this new viewpoint I could finally see the culprit. That pesky mandel bread pan had managed to squirm its way out the back again and wedge itself between the drawer and the wall. It's not really a baking pan at all, but the bottom of an old aluminum ice-cube tray, the kind they don't seem to make anymore now that plastic is around.

My mother used this oddball utensil to bake her famous mandel bread, a semi-sweet Russian pastry that was my "if I were lost on a desert island and could have only one thing to eat" food. She discovered it was just the right size to bake my favorite treat in her toaster oven so she didn't have to turn on the big oven and heat up the whole kitchen.

Using a broom handle, I fished for this sacred vessel, dented and stained from years of service, and gently dusted it off. Carefully, I placed it back in the drawer. Every year on my mother's birthday, I pull it out and bake mandel bread in my toaster oven.

For my daughter's wedding shower, in addition to her other gift, I gave her a set of old and dented aluminum ice cube trays that I had been saving for years. I included a recipe card with her grandmother's mandel bread recipe, so she could carry on the tradition of love and good eating.

*From* In My Mothers Kitchen: An Introduction to the Healing Power of Reminiscence *by Robin A. Edgar (Tree House Enterprises, 2003)*

---

A professional writer for over thirty years, **Robin A. Edgar** writes profiles and art reviews for publications such as *The Charlotte Observer, Charlotte Magazine,* and *Our State Magazine*. A successful workshop facilitator and keynote speaker, Ms. Edgar teaches reminiscence-writing workshops throughout the United States and overseas based on her book, *In My Mother's Kitchen: An Introduction to the Healing Power of Reminiscence*. Her most recent project, Personal Legacies: Surviving the Great Depression, captured oral histories in a book (CPCC Press), an exhibit at the Charlotte Museum of History, and a documentary with PBS affiliate, WTVI.

# *Grandma Sandra's Mandel Bread*

### Ingredients

| | |
|---|---|
| 2 | cups self-rising flour |
| ¾–1 | cup sugar, to taste |
| ¼ | cup oil |
| 2 | eggs |
| ¼ | teaspoon vanilla or almond extract |
| | Nuts (almonds or walnuts) and chocolate chips (as desired) |
| | Jelly, sour cream, or yogurt, as needed |

### Preparation

Preheat the oven to 350°F.

Sift the flour and sugar into a bowl. Add the remaining ingredients, and blend them until smooth. The batter should be the consistency of your ear lobe. If it is too dry, add some jelly, sour cream, or yogurt. Place the batter in 2 greased pans, and bake at 350°F. for 30 minutes.

Cool the bread, then slice it. Place the slices flat on a cookie sheet, and bake again at 350°F. for 10 minutes. Turn them after 5 minutes so that both sides are golden brown.

Makes 24 slices.

### Tips and Notes

To be true to Grandma Sandra's recipe, bake the mandel bread in old-fashioned aluminum ice-cube trays (discard the dividers that separate the cubes). If you do not have ice-cube trays, divide the batter into two 8x4-inch loaf pans.

If you don't have self-rising flour, add 2 teaspoons of baking powder and ¼ teaspoon of salt to 2 cups of regular flour.

# *Delight in the Differences*

**Valerie Lima**

Growing up in a culturally diverse family presented varied food experiences. Add to that our religious differences and living in the suburbs of New York City to fully understand the multiplicity of dishes.

My German Catholic maternal grandmother married my Russian Jewish grandfather. Their son married the daughter of a West Virginia Baptist minister, while my mother married into an English/Scottish/French family where my father's oldest brother and his wife were Catholic, his sister and her husband were Christian Scientists, and another brother was an atheist. Yet another brother and his wife were humanists, and another sister and my father were Protestants.

Every Easter when I was growing up, my family and my mother's brother's family would travel by car to my maternal grandparents' apartment in Queens. After everyone arrived, we would all climb the stairs to the roof for pictures before we kids could get our new Easter clothes dirty. Everyone would be up there waiting as my grandfather would adjust, focus, re-adjust and re-focus the lens. We would fidget, smelling the tar roof, listening to the church bells ringing across the street, and looking across the tops of the building and down to the street where city buses passed. Finally, pictures taken, we climbed back down to the apartment and searched for the Easter eggs and baskets my grandmother had hidden. Then we all enjoyed a traditional baked ham dinner with all the trimmings and, always available, matzo.

I grew up thinking that eating hard-boiled Easter eggs with buttered matzo was normal, as was eating German sauerbraten one day and Russian borscht the next. English roast beef and Yorkshire pudding followed by the next day's Jewish chicken soup with matzo dumplings. Pork chops with mint jelly or beef stroganoff with sour cream, a turkey leg or beef tongue, and so on.

One of my favorites was the challah my mother made, a Jewish yeast bread that's delicious with anything or by itself. She prepared it to accompany the things we ate that were not expected with Jewish Sabbath bread, like lasagna—one of my favorite combinations I still use for my adult children and grandchildren.

One of the advantages of the recipe my mother used was it provided two loaves, plenty for the seven of us growing up and then for the extended family. When I first married and baked the challah myself, I remembered the recipe called for eight cups of flour by thinking of one cup for each of the people in my birth family and one for my new husband.

The smell of the challah baking on a snowy winter's day or for any Sunday dinner, the sight of the braided loaves sprinkled with poppy seeds, the taste of the warm sweet bread with butter, the feel of the crunchy crust against the soft middle, the sound of a serrated knife slicing—this engaged all my senses and continues to do so.

I added to my family's diversity by marrying an Italian who introduced me to sheep's head, *bracciole,* cardoon, and cannoli. We later became vegetarians, learning about the many uses of tofu and gluten. My oldest son married a woman from Spain who introduced me to paella. Since I moved to Arkansas twenty-three years ago, I have eaten chocolate gravy, cornbread stuffing, peanuts in a Pepsi bottle, fried pies, okra, hush puppies, and grits.

Foods, like people, are delightfully diverse. To prejudge either limits us and our experiences. But in any culture, bread is a staple. A home-grown tomato on a slice of homemade challah bread hits the spot in any language.

# Challah

### Ingredients

- 1 package yeast
- ¼ cup warm water
- 2 cups hot water
- 1 tablespoon sugar or honey
- 2 tablespoons canola oil
- 1 tablespoon salt
- 2 eggs
- 8 cups flour, up to half whole wheat
- Cornmeal

### Preparation

Dissolve the yeast in ¼ cup lukewarm water.

Pour the hot water over the salt, sugar or honey, and oil in a large mixing bowl. Let stand. When the hot water mixture is lukewarm, add the yeast mixture, then the beaten eggs.

Add 7 cups of the flour gradually, mixing it into the liquids. Dampen the countertop and place a two-foot section of waxed paper on top. (Slightly wetting the countertop helps to keep the waxed paper in place.) Sprinkle the remaining cup of flour on top of the waxed paper and place the dough on top. Knead the dough until smooth.

Spray or wipe cooking oil on the inside of a large clean mixing bowl and place the dough in the bowl. Cover the bowl with a towel and let it double in bulk for about 1 hour.

Divide the dough in half. Cut one half into 4 equal pieces. With your hands, roll each piece about 1½ inches thick. Braid 3 pieces and place them on a cornmeal-sprinkled cookie sheet. Cut the remaining piece into 3 equal pieces, hand roll them, and braid them together. Place this on top of the larger braid to complete the loaf.

Repeat with the other half of the dough to form a second loaf.

Brush the loaves with water and sprinkle them with poppy seeds. Bake for 10 minutes in a pre-heated 400°F. oven, then for 30 minutes at 350°F. Cool, slice, and enjoy.

Makes 2 loaves.

---

**Valerie Lima** lives in Northwest Arkansas where her twenty-three-year association with Washington Regional Hospice has afforded her the opportunity to utilize her writing for a monthly newsletter as well as for training and continuing education. She also enjoys spirituality, reading, gardening, and traveling. She has had a poem published in *Releasing Times* and memoirs published at *Taborri Press* and *Story Circle Journal*, with another due for publication in *Sage of Consciousness*.

# *Autumn Delights*

**Nancy J. Rigg**

The world outside the window of our cabin is glazed with hoarfrost. It looks like a fairy kingdom, shimmering in the cool light of a Rocky Mountain fall morning. Every branch, leaf, and pinecone, even each individual blade of grass, is magically etched with the most intricate and dainty ice lacework.

The fire in our Franklin stove crackles and wheezes, taking the morning chill out of the air. I wrap myself up in my fleece bathrobe and measure water into the coffee pot. Earl, already dressed and ready to tackle the world, dons his parka and kisses me lightly on the cheek before heading down the road five miles to the post office. Colorado, our feisty English springer spaniel, gleefully bounds after him. As they disappear into the fairy forest, I smile and think how lucky and spoiled I am to have a man who will go all the way to town and back to bring me the mail and the morning newspaper every day.

We are living in Heaven on a 650-acre ranch located sixty miles northwest of Denver in a mountain valley. With a longing to fulfill our writers' dream of solitude and creativity, Earl and I have rented a cabin overlooking the main lake. In exchange for reduced rent, we have agreed to feed and watch over a small herd of horses through the winter while we write full time. It is a dream come true after several years of working in hectic, stressful, city jobs.

I grew up in the Rocky Mountains and know the profound feeling of freedom you can experience in a place where open land stretches before you. But this is Earl's first experience living at high altitude. He's a city guy who grew up in the Washington, DC, area. I'm enjoying the newness of all this through Earl's eyes, as we chop firewood, stock the shelves with supplies for times of being snowbound, and wax the snowshoes and cross-country skis that will be needed to trek from our cabin to the barn where the hay is stored.

Earl, who towers over me at six-foot four, has chosen a dark corner of the cabin attic for his writing area. "I don't want any distractions," he announces when I question his choice. Earl is a focused, intense, determined, prolific writer. Little do we realize that the short stories and children's books that he hammers out on his electric typewriter over the next several months will become his "complete works."

My desk faces a wide picture window overlooking the lake. I want to be distracted as much as possible, to allow my young writer's soul to soar with the blue jays and nut hatches that argue over birdseed on our porch, to lose myself in the howling wind on a stormy night, to join the chorus of coyotes whose evensongs ring out nightly, to dance with all the tiny rainbows refracted by sunlight through a dozen or more lead crystals that I've hung in the windows. The joy of living in blessed solitude, buffered from the busy world by acres and acres of undeveloped

*Continues on page 26*

---

**Nancy J. Rigg** is a writer and filmmaker. Her fiancé, Earl Higgins, lost his life while rescuing a child who was swept away in a flash flood in 1980, just six weeks after Nancy and Earl moved from Colorado to Los Angeles. Happy memories are mixed into this special recipe.

# *Nancy's Zucchini or Pumpkin Bread*

## Ingredients

### Wet ingredients

| | |
|---|---|
| 1 | cup vegetable oil |
| 3 | cups (approx.) cooked pumpkin or fresh zucchini, peeled and sliced |
| 3 | eggs |
| 1½–2 | cups sugar, to taste |
| 3 | teaspoons vanilla |

### Dry ingredients

| | |
|---|---|
| 3 | cups flour |
| 1 | teaspoon baking soda |
| ½ | teaspoon baking powder |
| 1 | teaspoon ground nutmeg |
| 1 | teaspoon ground clove |
| 3 | teaspoons ground cinnamon |
| | Pinch of salt (optional) |

### Optional ingredients

| | |
|---|---|
| 1 | handful of hulled sunflower seeds |
| 1 | cup chopped walnuts |
| 1 | cup raisins |
| 1 | cup fresh cranberries |
| ½ | cup dried cranberries |
| 1 | cup bittersweet chocolate chips |

## Preparation

Preheat oven to 350°F. First, prepare the cooked pumpkin or raw zucchini.

**To prepare pumpkin:** Slice a sugar pumpkin or other tasty cooking pumpkin in half, and remove seeds. Place the pumpkin halves face down in a little water and either microwave or bake in the oven until soft. Allow the pumpkin to cool before peeling.

**To prepare zucchini:** Peel and slice enough fresh zucchini to yield 3–3½ cups.

**To prepare the bread batter:** Measure one cup of oil into a 5-cup blender jar; add ½ the pumpkin or zucchini slices and blend, adding more until you have a total of 3 cups of wet goo. Add eggs, vanilla, and sugar to this mixture and blend well. It will yield about 5 cups total of wet ingredients in the blender jar. Set aside.

Using a wooden spoon, mix the flour, baking soda, baking powder, and ground spices by hand in a large mixing bowl. Pour in wet ingredients and mix well. Add optional ingredients of your choice.

Hand mix everything together thoroughly, but don't overdo it. You want the batter moist but not overworked.

Pour the batter into greased loaf pans. Bake at 350°F. for about 1 hour in regular pans or 45 minutes in mini-pans. Prick the bread with a toothpick to see if it's done. It should be moist inside but not gooey or too sticky. Remove the bread from the pan and serve warm with butter or cream cheese.

Makes two 8½x4½-inch loaves or 6 mini-loaves.

## Tips and Notes

You may substitute up to ¼ cup rolled oats or wheat germ or bran for ¼ cup of flour to make a denser bread dough.

This is a wonderful holiday treat, starting at Halloween and lasting clear through the New Year!

The bread freezes well for later use. Wrap it tightly in aluminum foil and store it in a plastic freezer bag.

Continued from page 24

wildlands, is something I intend to embrace and enjoy fully.

I sip dark, fresh-brewed coffee and laugh when my gaze falls on a small basket that Earl has left on the counter. Hint, hint! About a half-dozen large, fresh zucchinis are lounging there beside a plump, orange sugar pumpkin. For such a young couple—Earl and I have been together only three years—autumn baking has already become an annual ritual for us. Earl loves the zucchini and pumpkin bread that I bake from scratch. I'll have just enough time to bake two loaves before he returns from town.

As the bread bakes, I toss a few extra sunflower seeds outside onto the patio where the noisy blue jays are waiting for their breakfast. With the sunshine, the fairy world is melting, and I pause to contemplate the impermanence of life. I want to cling forever to this moment, this life here in the mountains with Earl. I want to have children with him and raise them in a setting like this where they can thrive.

I want to get that zucchini bread out of the oven before it burns!

With two loaves of steaming zucchini bread ready to be liberated from the bread pans, I hear a little yap at the front door, as Earl and Colorado enter the cabin. Earl's ruggedly handsome face is flushed from the walk and his dark eyes shine with joy.

"Mmmmmmm!" he sighs. "That almost smells good enough to eat." We sit by the fire, savoring the full richness of each small bite. Fresh zucchini bread! With pumpkin bread to follow. There is no greater celebration of autumn and all its bounty.

# Slices

**Jazz Jaeschke**

3:00 a.m.
Kneading paws slice into my slumber
arousing me to slice into the banana bread
baked by you during an impromptu slice
out of your last night slice of this busy week
conjuring visions of you slicing at cutting board
whetting my appetite for slices of your kisses
tempting me to slice into *your* slumber!
3:30 a.m.

---

Actively retired, **Jazz Jaeschke** facilitates writing circles, including the SCN Internet Poetry Circle, and devotes many hours to her journal and poetry. Hiking, especially into canyons, is a competing passion. Her ever-present camera records scenes along the way for spinning into poems when the pace slows. Jazz lives in Austin, Texas, with too many cats and just the right man who enjoys cooking while she's writing. Her only critical shortage is time.

# *Wake Me Up! Banana Bread*

### Ingredients

| | |
|---|---|
| 6–8 | fresh oranges |
| ½ | cup butter, soft but not melted |
| 1 | cup sugar |
| 2 | large eggs |
| 3 | nicely ripe bananas, mashed |
| 1 | cup unbleached flour |
| 1 | cup whole wheat flour |
| 1 | teaspoon baking soda |
| 1 | teaspoon pure vanilla |
| ¾ | cup chopped pecans |
| ½ | cup dried cranberries |

### Preparation

Preheat the oven to 350°F.

With a zester, vegetable peeler, paring knife, or wood rasp, scrape the oranges' colored layer to obtain about ½ cup orange zest. Avoid scraping into the underlying white pith.

Cream the butter and sugar. Add the next 8 ingredients one at a time in the order listed, making sure each is thoroughly blended before adding the next. If using an electric mixer, stir in the pecans and cranberries by hand. Stir in the orange zest.

Pour the batter into a greased 8½x4½-inch loaf pan. (Do not flour the pan.) Bake for 1 hour at 350°F.

Test for doneness; continue baking for 5 to 15 minutes until a knife blade inserted in the center comes out clean.

Makes one 8½x4½-inch loaf.

### Tips and Notes

Use raw sugar instead of white sugar, for a richer flavor.

Serve warm for breakfast with butter, or cool the bread, wrap in aluminum foil, and deliver to your best friend.

Stores for several days (if hidden).

Slices better when cool; deliciously crumbly when hot.

The batter can be baked as muffins; reduce the cooking time.

What to do with the left-over oranges? I usually eat a couple while the bread is baking and put the rest in a baggie in the fridge for later. You can even juice the oranges and reserve the juice before scraping the zest; orange juice goes well with this breakfast bread.

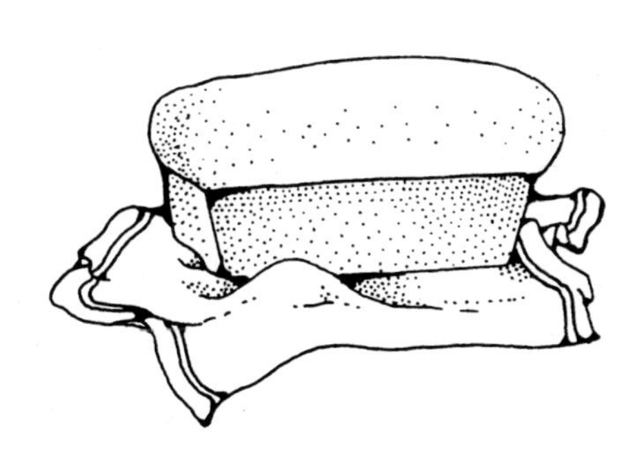

# Grandmother's Date Nut Bread

**Anne K. Waldron**

When I was a young girl, my mother would periodically hold her "Ward Belmont Tea." Ward Belmont was a junior college in Nashville, Tennessee. Mother kept in touch with a group of other 1926 graduates who also lived in New York City. Although my mother worked in vocational guidance in Manhattan, our family lived in Queens. My father was a Baptist minister.

A day or so before the tea, Mother prepared her mother's recipes—date nut bread and frozen ambrosia. The morning of the tea, Mother made cucumber and deviled-ham tea sandwiches with white bread, the crusts trimmed. She wrapped the sandwiches in a damp tea towel and chilled them in the refrigerator. Then she sliced the date nut bread, spread it with softened cream cheese, and made small sandwiches, which she also chilled in a damp tea towel.

My sister and I helped set the dining room table with the silver tea and coffee service, the turquoise and yellow plates and cups with saucers, Haviland china, and her sterling silver spoons and forks. In the afternoon, right before the guests were to arrive, Mother arranged the sandwiches on plates and cut the frozen salad into small squares. The salad was crushed pineapple, bananas, chopped walnuts, and maraschino cherries, folded into whipped cream and frozen in ice-cube trays. The time of day was late afternoon; candles were lit, and the world seemed beautiful with those ladies so excited to see each other and making a fuss over me and my sister.

In about 1959, after my husband Jack and I had moved into our first house with three small children, I asked my mother for the date nut bread recipe. My grandmother's recipe makes one large loaf, the size of a standard loaf pan. I usually double the recipe and make two large loaves, one to keep and one to give away. For the past thirty-five years, I have always made that date nut bread on Christmas Eve and sometimes the week before, depending on how many loaves I wanted to give away. The aroma of date nut bread baking always brings my heart to Christmas.

When we lived in Hawaii, from 1962 to 1967, I started making three loaves from a double recipe and used chopped macadamia nuts instead of walnuts. At that time macadamia nuts were inexpensive and gave a new flavor to the bread. In about 1964, the *Honolulu Advertiser* ran a recipe contest. I sent in my date nut bread recipe and said it was an old family recipe that dated back at least to my grandmother, in Vincennes, Indiana, where my mother grew up. Lo and behold, my recipe was printed in the paper with a note about my grandmother.

When we moved back to West Chester, Pennsylvania, in 1967, I switched back to walnuts and started making more and more loaves. My date nut bread became popular. Some friends counted on having it for their Christmas breakfast. Eventually, I started making five loaves to a double recipe and making it two double-recipe bowls at a

---

**Anne Waldron** and her husband Jack have loved being married for almost fifty-three years. They are fortunate to have five children and seven grandchildren, plus good health. Except for a wonderful five-year sojourn in Honolulu, they have lived in West Chester, Pennsylvania. Anne enjoys reflective writing, book groups, and playing bridge, and she has given several workshops using Susan Wittig Albert's book, *Writing from Life*.

# Carrie's Date Nut Bread

### Ingredients

| | |
|---|---|
| 16 | ounces (approx.) chopped dates |
| 1 | stick (or 4 ounces) butter |
| 1½–2 | cups sugar (to taste) |
| 2 | teaspoons baking soda |
| 2 | cups boiling water |
| 2 | eggs, stirred in a bowl |
| 2 | cups chopped walnuts or macadamia nuts |
| 2 | teaspoons vanilla |
| ½–¾ | teaspoon salt |
| 3 | cups flour, sifted |

### Preparation

Preheat the oven to 350°F.

Put the first 4 ingredients in a large bowl. Pour 2 cups boiling water over them. Mix gently and let stand for about 15 minutes.

Grease two 9x5x3-inch loaf pans and put strips of waxed paper in the bottom and up over the ends of the pans, then lightly grease the waxed paper.

Add the eggs, nuts, vanilla, and salt to the cooling mixture. Gently fold in the flour with a large spatula, turning over the dough as little as possible until the flour is evenly incorporated into the mixture. Pour the dough into the loaf pans.

Bake at 350°F. for approximately 40 minutes. Turn the oven temperature down to 325°F. and bake for another 15 minutes, checking every 5 minutes to see if the bread is done.

Cool the bread for 10 minutes in the loaf pans. Remove from the pans and wrap in foil, leaving ends open, for another 20 minutes.

Makes two large 9x5x3-inch loaves.

### Tips and Notes

This double recipe makes 2 large loaves, 3 medium loaves, or 5 mini-loaves. The recipe can also be halved to make 1 large loaf.

Baking time may vary with different size loaves. Always check progress after 40 minutes. Insert a knife to test. When it comes out clean, the bread is done.

---

time, making ten small loaves.

One year, I thought, *Making date nut bread is too much work. Who needs date nut bread, anyway?* However, as Christmas neared, I rushed out and bought the ingredients and went to work. The realization came over me how much I really loved to make this bread and share it with friends, every Christmas. Two years ago, I even took pictures of the process and included them in a PowerPoint presentation with the recipe for my children.

I believe that the key to this particularly delicious and moist bread is soaking the dates in boiling water, along with sugar, water, and butter, for fifteen or twenty minutes, which makes the finished loaf a nice dark brown.

Since I had always thought of this recipe as my grandmother's, imagine my surprise when, after my mother's death, my sister Carolyn informed me that mother got the recipe from the *New York Times*!

# *Falling in Love with Panettone*

**Arlene Howard**

"Come in now," my mom called. Reluctantly, I stopped playing hopscotch.

"You're old enough to go to the store by yourself. Get a box of fresh ravioli for dinner."

We lived on 40th Avenue in San Francisco. Down the street and around the corner was a small Italian delicatessen. I remember fresh pasta, cold cuts, crusty loaves of Larraburu sourdough bread, and barrels of candy.

"*Ciao*. What does your mama want today?"

"A big box of fresh ravioli."

"*Aspetta.*" (Wait a minute.)

The Italian man who owned the delicatessen placed two dozen fresh ravioli in a large flat white cardboard box and tied it with string. "For you, *bambina*."

I handed him three dimes and a nickel.

"Take a root beer candy from the barrel," he told me.

*I like being eight,* I thought.

We had fresh ravioli that night and many more nights that year.

Soon it was Christmastime. The delicatessen was filled with all kinds of treats. On Christmas Eve, the delicatessen owner gave me a large golden cellophane wrapped package.

"Take it home to your Mama."

"What is it? What is it, Mom? Open it. Open it."

"Oh, my. *Panettone di Natale*. We'll have this special Italian Christmas bread after dinner. Wait till you taste it." My first bite of that delicious confection was the beginning of my love affair with panettone.

In 1986, my husband Alan, our nine-year-old daughter Allyson, and I arrived in Milan in early December for a four-month stay. On the first evening, we drove around and around the city to get our bearings.

"Alan, stop!" I shouted. "There's a *panetteria*."

In the window, round loaves of panettone were bedecked in yards of clear cellophane and red, green, and white ribbons. My husband, who wasn't really fond of stopping suddenly in traffic in the middle of a strange city, did find a place to pull over. Good food is a heady persuader. "I'll meet you at the corner by the green clock," Alan said.

We bought the most beautiful *Panettone di Natale*. We smiled as we walked to the corner. No Alan. Where was he? Fifteen minutes ticked by slowly on the hands of the big clock, then thirty, and then forty-five. It was cold. It began to drizzle.

"He's lost and he won't ask for directions," I thought.

After one hour, my daughter cried out, "Oh look. There's Dad."

I wasn't smiling as I got in the car. "Where did you go?" I demanded.

*Continues on page 32*

---

**Arlene Howard**, an SCN member since 2007, lives in Rancho Mirage, California, with her husband Alan, her Saint Bernard Nala, and twenty-year-old cat Katisha. A retired librarian, Arlene writes a travel column "Desert Destinations" for *The Desert Woman*. Writing, visiting her daughter, quilting, watching old movies, and gardening with her husband keep her busy.

# *Panettone di Natale*

## Ingredients

### Dough

| | |
|---|---|
| ⅓ | cup warm water |
| 1 | tablespoon yeast |
| ¼ | cup flour |
| 1 | teaspoon sugar |
| ½ | cup milk, lukewarm |
| ⅓ | cup butter, soft |
| ⅓ | cup sugar |
| 2 | eggs plus 1 egg yolk, beaten |
| ½ | teaspoon salt |
| 1 | teaspoon grated lemon peel |
| ½ | teaspoon vanilla |
| 3½–4 | cups flour, enough to form a soft dough |
| ½ | cup golden raisins |
| ½ | cup candied citron |

### Topping

| | |
|---|---|
| 1 | egg yolk mixed with 1 teaspoon water |
| 2 | tablespoons sliced almonds |
| 2 | tablespoons powdered sugar |

## Preparation

Mix the water, yeast, ¼ cup flour, and sugar together in a medium bowl. Let the mixture rest until it bubbles, about 15 minutes. Combine the milk, butter, sugar, beaten eggs, salt, lemon peel, and vanilla in a large bowl. Add the yeast mixture. Using a mixer with a dough hook or mixing by hand with a large wooden spoon, add the flour about ½ cup at a time until the dough forms a soft ball.

Knead the dough for 5–10 minutes, adding enough flour to form a soft, not sticky, ball. Place the dough in a large bowl, and cover it with waxed paper and a damp towel. Let the dough rise until it has doubled in size, about 2 hours.

Punch the dough down on a board and roll it out into a 9x12-inch rectangle. Sprinkle on the raisins and citron. Roll the dough and stretch and shape it into a 15-inch roll. Place it in a very well-buttered tube or Bundt pan.

Brush the top with the egg yolk–water mixture, and sprinkle with sliced almonds. Let the dough rise again until it is double.

Bake at 400°F. for 10 minutes, then reduce the oven temperature to 350°F. and continue baking for 35 minutes. The bread will feel firm when done.

Remove bread from pan. Dust the top with powdered sugar, and let the bread cool before slicing.

Makes one 9-inch round loaf.

### Tips and Notes

You may add 1 tablespoon of gluten with the flour, if desired, for a lighter-textured bread.

If you prefer to use a bread machine, mix the water, yeast, ¼ cup flour, and sugar, and let the mixture rest until it bubbles, about 15 minutes. Put the yeast mixture and the remaining ingredients, except the raisins and citron, into the bread machine pan. Set the machine on the dough setting; it will beep in about 2 hours. When the cycle is complete, take the dough out of the bread machine. Punch the dough down on a board. Follow the directions above to form the dough and bake.

*Continued from page 30*

"The *polizia* said, '*Uscire di qui.*' (Get out of here.) The only way I knew how to find you was to back track to the apartment and start over. There are a lot of one-way streets. It is opening night at La Scala. You know, you're lucky I got back here at all!" He was frustrated. Very. I was mad. Very. On reflection, I am not sure why I was.

Not much was said on the ride back to the apartment. Soon we were there. After dinner we opened the beautiful package and ate the most wonderful panettone. It was perfect with the traditional drink of Asti Spumante. We began to giggle; soon we were laughing—at what is now known in our family as "The Lost Corner" story. It has gotten much funnier over the years.

When I was a young bride, I made panettone from a recipe found in *Gourmet, Volume II*. The cookbook had been a birthday gift along with a box of Betty Crocker cake mix from my husband when he was my boyfriend. I have always wondered if the gift, wrapped in a brown paper bag, was a test.

During the first years, I kneaded the panettone by hand; then I got a KitchenAid mixer with a dough hook. Finally, I bought a bread machine and dumped everything into the pan. Now I use the bread machine to do the hard work—the mixing and kneading and first rising. After shaping it, I bake it in the oven. Over time, the recipe has evolved, but it remains a delicious, rich, buttery Milanese Christmas bread filled with citron and golden raisins and adorned with sugar and almonds.

Making *Panettone di Natale* each Christmas brings back memories of growing up in San Francisco, the "lost corner" in Milan, our holiday parties, and visiting Venice another December. The memories fill me and my family with smiles and laughter. Perhaps you will fall in love with panettone, too.

---

## *Culinary Detours*

**A Writing Prompt**

Have you ever taken a detour or broken a journey to find or sample a local delicacy or speciality? Have you ever gone searching for a special food or an ingredient and gotten lost along the way? Remember the sights, sounds, smells, and tastes of your most memorable culinary detour and the adventure that went with it. Write the story of this journey.

# Light Dishes

## Soups, Salads, Sides, and Vegetarian Dishes

# *Aunt Bertha's Lake Hotel Restaurant*

**Sharon Blumberg**

It was a sad moment in time for a thirty-eight-year tradition in Gary, Indiana, when Bertha (Deutsch) Simon locked the doors for the last time at the Lake Hotel Restaurant on Washington Street in 1968. It was also sad for the many customers who enjoyed her excellent food.

When Bertha first came to the United States from Austria-Hungary, she could not speak English, let alone cook up a bowl of soup. Little did Bertha realize that when she offered to help her brother, the late Adolph Deutsch, to manage the Lake Hotel Restaurant for two weeks, that she would still be running it thirty-eight years later. Before that time, she had been a buyer in the art department of a Gary store when she volunteered for what was to become her future career. With $167 in the bank in 1930, Bertha began to learn the restaurant business and to run it more than successfully as a family enterprise.

Customers stopped by just for a cup of coffee and to take part in a friendly conversation with Bertha. Families came for meals in an ambiance that was warm and personal because Bertha took a special interest in her customers. People from businesses and organizations dined at the restaurant on a regular basis. Business was conducted, friendships developed, and diets were broken over the delicious homemade dishes.

Prices and the cost of living were very different than they are today. Waitresses worked hard for long hours. They earned eight dollars a week, and they held true to a wonderful work ethic. Most of the workers who were with Bertha when she locked the doors for the last time had been with her for over twenty years.

The restaurant became famous, especially for its soups—split pea, lentil, potato, chicken giblet, matzo ball, egg drop, and navy bean (which just happened to be made the same way it was made in the U.S. Senate). One could order a generous slice of homemade pie for ten cents, and for another nickel, you could have it á la mode. If you had thirty cents to spend, you could order a plate lunch with soup, chocolate or tapioca pudding, and a beverage with your entrée.

My mother used to take my sister and me to eat lunch at the Lake Hotel Restaurant when we were small children. We often used to eat there after going shopping in downtown Gary. My favorite dish was the rich, navy bean soup, and I loved the savory, pink Thousand Island dressing. These were treats to my taste buds.

Shortly before I reached my twenty-fifth birthday, I got married. I once again became acquainted with Bertha through my husband's family. She was his great-aunt, his mother's aunt. Bertha had a cute sense of humor. My husband Reuben used to say to her at family get-togethers, "Aunt Bertha, smile for the camera, but don't break it."

She would laugh as she would retort, "You are so full of baloney."

Her joy was grand at my first family dinner when she discovered that I remembered meeting her and dining at her restaurant. Our joyous encounter was the beginning of a new family friendship for a number of years to come.

When she passed away in 1995, it was a mournful day for her family and her numerous friends and acquaintances. In addition, it was the end of a long and wonderful life for Aunt Bertha. Even though she was well into her nineties, she was and still is deeply missed. But one important fact rings true. She left a legacy of beloved memories behind from another era not long past.

# Dried Bean Soup

### Ingredients

| | |
|---|---|
| ¼ | cup dried navy, kidney, lima, or marrow beans |
| ¼ | pound ham or salt pork, or a ham bone |
| ½ | bay leaf |
| 3–4 | peppercorns |
| 3 | whole cloves |
| 4 | cups boiling water |
| 1 | carrot, diced |
| 3 | ribs celery with leaves, chopped |
| ½ | onion, sliced |

### Optional ingredients

| | |
|---|---|
| 1 | clove garlic, minced |
| ⅛ | teaspoon saffron |
| ½ | cup freshly cooked mashed potatoes |
| ½ | cup chopped sorrel |
| | Chives or parsley, chopped, for garnish |

### Preparation

Soak the beans overnight in water to cover.

In a large pot, combine the drained beans, ham, bay leaf, peppercorns, and cloves, and cover with boiling water. Cook the soup slowly until the beans are soft, about 2½–3 hours. For the last 30 minutes add the carrots, celery, and onion. Add the garlic, saffron, mashed potatoes, and sorrel, if desired.

Remove and mince the meat. Remove and discard the ham bone, if used. Put the soup through a food mill, blender, or sieve. Thin the soup, if necessary, with boiling water or milk. Adjust the seasoning according to taste. Serve with the meat and chopped chives or parsley.

Makes 4 cups.

### Tips and Notes

If you use marrow beans and add the optional mashed potato, you will come close to reproducing the famous United States Senate Bean Soup.

**(Thousand Island Dressing)**

### Ingredients

| | |
|---|---|
| 1 | 8-ounce can beets, sliced and chopped |
| 1 | small pickle, chopped |
| 1 | hard boiled egg, chopped |
| 1 | 12-ounce bottle chili sauce |
| 1 | pint mayonnaise |

### Preparation

Mix all of the ingredients together thoroughly by hand or by food processor. Refrigerate and enjoy!

### Tips and Notes

The original recipe calls for Hines brand chili sauce.

Makes a wonderful dressing for a simple salad of chopped Romaine lettuce.

---

**Sharon Blumberg** resides in Munster, Indiana, with her husband and dog. She has a daughter who recently graduated from college and a son who is in his second year of college. She has been a Spanish teacher for the last twelve years at Parker Junior High in Flossmoor, Illinois. In her spare time, she is aspiring to see her second career, as a freelance writer, flourish.

# *Slow Food: A Personal History*

**Carol Ann Sayle**

In the 1950s, my mother, Little Dove, spent a lot of time in the green kitchen of our house on the outskirts of San Antonio, even though she hated to cook. To encourage her in her often-cheerless efforts, my father, Chief, bought her a special convenience: a self-standing roaster to be used primarily for cooking Sunday dinners. The rest of the week, it could double as a breadbox. Chief liked versatile things that could pull their own weight. Money was tight, but if delicious meals were to be the result, he was willing to strain his budget to provide the equipment.

Little Dove liked the luxury roaster, felt emboldened by it, and in it, she perfected her famous pot roast and succulent ham. Even the Thanksgiving turkey went into the rectangular pot, as long as the bird was small enough for the domed lid to close.

On Sundays, we were hustled off to church and Sunday school, secure in the knowledge that the meat of the moment, accompanied by its potatoes, was roasting to tender perfection. As long as we could demonstrate that we did not fight or snore during the sermon, we knew we could feast.

Once home from church, Little Dove prepared the rest of the meal—canned green peas and pickled beets, typically with a salad of whitish iceberg lettuce.

We all sat down to eat together at the green table in the green kitchen. There was no television set at the meal. All of us kids were admonished to clean our plates, and if we didn't do it in a timely fashion, we sat there until we managed either to eat everything or to hide the undesirable portion in a napkin in our laps. We never quite figured how much time was proper for food consumption. Even though Dove, her roaster, and someone's far-flung factories had spent a lot of time preparing the food, and even though my brother Bill and I would later spend a lot of time washing and drying dishes, the meal was often a race. Chief in particular ate at a rapid pace, which indicated, just as burping does in some societies, that he truly enjoyed the repast. My brother adapted to this model, which perturbed Little Dove no end. She wanted her food savored; she wanted wonderful conversation; she wanted our digestion to be tranquil. She didn't often get what she wanted.

"Bill Junior, *slow down*!" she'd say. He tried to comply, but he was a born speed eater.

Little Dove was ahead of her time in some respects, but she wasn't into vegetable gardening. Chief had to work two jobs, which left her with little time for extra activities. That's what she said, but I suspect that it was just too easy to open a can. So, while the meat we ate was from Texas sources, the vegetables were from who-knows-where. Much later on when I asked her why we'd eaten so much from cans, she rationalized: "We couldn't afford frozen."

I didn't learn to cook from my mother. In fact I didn't learn to cook until 1982 when my husband Larry and I began to grow our own food at our first farm in Gause, in Milam County. The vegetables were amazing. Finally mustard greens without the can! (Yes, those horrid-

---

**Carol Ann Sayle** is an organic vegetable/fruit farmer with over sixteen years of interesting experience. Following a successful art career of twenty years, she considers Boggy Creek Farm, the farm she co-owns with her husband in Austin, Texas, to be an eternal subject and palette. www.boggycreekfarm.com

tasting, soggy strings always wound up in the napkin in my lap. Do you blame me?) And the first year we farmed commercially, we grew a lot of eggplant. I figured out nine ways to fix it, ruining any chance of Larry ever being fond of it.

"Again?" he'd ask in disbelief.

"Well," I'd plead, "we *have* to eat it—we can't sell it all!"

Much of the food we grew we'd never eaten before, but we fell in love with something new at every harvest. I remember sautéing greens, chopped onions, and garlic in an iron skillet, anointing them with balsamic vinegar, sprinkling them with feta cheese, and sitting back and sighing about how good it all was!

It was amazing the difference between something that was growing out back—minutes from the kitchen—and the normal, well-traveled, grocery-store fare. The vegetables we grew were fresh, not weary. There was still a hum of life that transferred itself to our bodies, made us strong, gave us energy, and inspired us to grow more, for ourselves and for our friends at the farm stand. We were doing "Slow Food" and we didn't even know it.

*This story first appeared in* EdibleAustin *magazine, Summer 2007 issue. Reprinted with permission. www.edibleaustin.com*

### Ingredients

| | |
|---|---|
| 2 | cups vegetable stock or water |
| 2 | cups sorrel leaves |
| ½–1 | cup chopped onion |
| 4 | tablespoons butter |
| 4–6 | medium potatoes, peeled and thinly sliced |
| 1 | cup milk, half and half, or soy milk |
| | Salt and pepper to taste |
| | Dill or chervil, chopped, for garnish |

### Preparation

Heat stock in a medium pan. Melt the butter in a skillet. Stew the sorrel and onion in the butter for about 6 minutes. Add the sorrel and onion and the potatoes to the simmering stock. Simmer, covered for 25 minutes. Pour the soup into a blender and blend on high until very smooth.

Reheat the blended soup in a clean pan. Adjust seasoning. Add the milk or cream. Serve warm or cold.

Serves 2.

*This recipe first appeared in* Eating in Season: Recipes from Boggy Creek Farm, *by Carol Ann Sayle. 1999. Reprinted with permission. www.boggycreekfarm.com*

# Two Hundred Thirty-One Independence Days

**Susan Myrick**

I remind myself, amid the picnic hot dogs, of the first Independence Day in 1776, over two hundred years ago. The Reformation and the Enlightenment that gave birth to our nation inspire me to explore and study in greater detail those remarkable times. This past spring I located the names of ancestors who fought in the Revolutionary War. There were three: two Means men and one Mayes, all Presbyterian Scotsmen. I once read that the American Revolution was called the Scottish Revolution at the time because the democratic-thinking Scots fiercely led the fight against the despised hierarchical English.

During my childhood, we celebrated Independence Days with democratic devotion and a fierce spread of picnic foods. Our family might gather at my grandparents' house or pack a picnic and find a picnic table in Forest Park, the site of St. Louis' World Fair.

Our picnics included my parents, hot dogs, two sisters, both sets of grandparents, potato salad, ham, fried chicken, frosted flag cake, fruit pies, pork and beans, deviled eggs, slaw, sliced garden-fresh tomatoes, fresh peaches, watermelon, lemonade, and more often than not, an out-of-town relative or two. The meal was a celebration of our garden's delicious abundance as much as it was the nation's independence. And unlike routine meals, we had the liberty to choose our favorite foods. I went for the beans, eggs, and fresh vegetables, but only as a precursor to the cake.

After feasting, our family headed for the fireworks displays in the football field at Washington University. I endured the ground displays until the booms and sparkles of the sky phase took over at dusk.

I remember the last traditional Independence Day fireworks celebration that marked the point between home life and my own independence. I lived in the dorm while finishing my master's degree in science education. I had a teaching contract for the fall in my desk and a love in my heart. He was Jay, and he was heading for law school at the University of Michigan. I was to teach junior high science near Washington, DC, a city in which so many young women, fresh out of college, were comfortable beginning their adult lives.

That summer was among the hottest on record in St. Louis. The electric company rationed air conditioning, so students dragged themselves about the campus, melting into soppy pools of matter in classrooms and library carrels.

On July fourth that year, the temperature soared and would not, did not, cool below a hundred degrees, even that night. The fireworks seemed to warm the air still another degree. If time was sending us off to new lives, so was the fiery summer burning away the hometown phase of our lives.

Three years later, Jay and I were married and spending our first summer in Chicago. Living away from the extended families, we began to create our own customs around a family of good friends. A new tradition can be whipped fluffy with nuggets of the old until what is new becomes old and cherished.

# Garden Tomato Soup

### Ingredients

- 2 ounces unsalted butter
- 1 large onion, peeled and chopped (sweet onion, if you can get one)
- 2½ pounds potatoes, peeled and chopped or sliced
- 3 pounds fresh tomatoes
- 1 scant cup water
- ¼ teaspoon white pepper
- 2 tablespoons sugar
- Salt to taste
- Heavy cream or milk, to taste

### Preparation

Melt the butter in a large pot. Add the onions and sauté until golden brown.

Add the tomatoes and potatoes. Add water to just cover the tomatoes and potatoes. Less is better because you can adjust the liquid at the end. Bring to a full boil for 30 minutes. Continuously remove all residue that comes to the top using a ladle. Don't worry if you take some of the soup in the process.

Remove and puree the tomatoes and potatoes in a food processor or blender. Return the puree to the tomato broth in the pot. Bring to the boil again. Add sugar and salt and pepper to taste to balance the acidity of the tomatoes and add a little spice. If there are any chunks or large pieces of potato left, you will have to pass them through the processor again.

Let the broth cool. Heat only the amount of broth you are going to serve. Then add cream or milk to taste and reheat. Serve immediately.

Serves 6–8

### Tips and Notes

You can use canned tomatoes in place of fresh. Reserve the juice.

You may refrigerate the soup base for later. Remember to add milk or cream to the soup right before serving.

---

**Susan Myrick** lives in suburban Chicago with her husband, an inventor and lawyer, in a house on the village historical registry. Built in 1877, the house stimulates her interest in memory and history. Before retirement she taught high-school science, photography, and cooking. She is a mother of two and a new grandmother. Her memoirs have appeared in the *Story Circle Journal, Northwestern University OLLI Journal,* and in an anthology, *Gifts from Our Grandmothers*.

# *Roberta's Blues Plate Specials*

**Mary M. Elizabeth**

My grandmother was an excellent cook. She taught none of her skills to my mother. My mother might have thought she would eventually hire a cook but my father, a successful dentist, died and that possibility died, too.

My mother's favorite kitchen utensil was the can opener. Unlike our cat, my brothers and I did not run salivating to the kitchen when we heard its soft, repetitive grind-grind-grind. Back then, can openers were not recognizable by their electric buzz.

Our major food groups came from the Campbell Company, Libby's, Del Monte, Dole, Uncle Ben, Aunt Jemima, Van Kamps, Bird's Eye, and Swanson's.

Casseroles were my mother's specialties. Chicken and rice casserole based on Campbell's Cream of Chicken or Cream of Mushroom soups. A spaghetti casserole with squares of Kraft American cheese on top. They weren't too bad. On a par with our school cafeteria food or just a notch down.

She made minute steaks and meat loaf. Despite the tenderizing process that the minute steaks went through, when my mother fried them they were tough and tasteless with a little crunchy edge. We ate a lot of Peter Pan white bread, crunchy Skippy peanut butter, and Highland Potato Chips.

Probably the main ingredient in my mother's cooking was resentment. She didn't enjoy cooking, even her own minimalist school. She begrudged the time it took at the end of the day. When any of us made the mistake of asking what we were having for dinner that night she'd slam a spoon or spatula against the stove and shout angrily, "Food!"

She hated the routine we developed of eating on TV trays in the living room. We ate in front of the TV, even though the evening news was the only thing on at the time. We ate casseroles and minute steaks through the civil rights movement and the Viet Nam War.

We always spent Thanksgiving and Christmas at my grandmother's. My mother made sure of that.

---

**Mary M. Elizabeth** was born in Iowa City, Iowa. She was known for her poetry during high school. She was educated at Grinnell College, the University of New Mexico, and the University of Iowa, as well as in numerous types of employment including operating an overhead crane at a factory in Iowa City for two years. She facilitates a Story Circle writing group and specializes in laughter.

### Ingredients

| | |
|---|---|
| 4 | tablespoons olive oil |
| 3 | medium leeks |
| 4 | garlic cloves, minced |
| 2 | medium carrots, peeled |
| 2 | stalks celery |
| 8 | cups chicken broth |
| | Salt |
| 1 | teaspoon whole black peppercorns |
| 3 | sprigs each fresh thyme and parsley |
| 12 | green beans, trimmed |
| 4 | medium zucchini |
| 1 | ripe tomato, peeled and seeded |

### Pistou

| | |
|---|---|
| 6 | medium garlic cloves, peeled |
| 6 | tomatoes, peeled, seeded, & chopped |
| 4–6 | tablespoons extra-virgin olive oil |
| 30 | fresh basil leaves, washed and dried |

### Preparation

Prepare the vegetables. Trim the dark green parts from the leeks and discard, keeping just the light green and white parts. Wash and cut all the vegetables into ½-inch pieces.

In a large saucepan, heat the olive oil over medium-high heat. Add the leeks and sauté until they just start to turn translucent, about 3 minutes. Add the garlic and sauté about 1 minute more. Add the carrots and celery and continue sautéing 3–4 minutes more. Pour the stock into the pan, bring it to a boil, and reduce the heat to maintain a simmer. Season with a generous pinch of salt.

Tie the peppercorns, thyme, and parsley in a square of cheesecloth, using kitchen string. Add this bouquet garni to the pan. Stir in the beans, zucchini, and tomato. Continue simmering until the vegetables are tender, about 30 minutes.

Meanwhile, make the pistou by blending all the pistou ingredients together in a food processor until they form a smooth paste.

When the soup is ready, remove and discard the bouquet garni. Stir ⅓ of the pistou into the saucepan. Taste the soup and adjust the seasoning.

Ladle the soup into individual heated serving bowls. Serve immediately, passing the remaining pistou for each person to add more, to taste. Serves 6–8.

## Bittersweet Green Salad

### Ingredients

| | |
|---|---|
| 1 | cup walnut or pecan halves |
| 3 | tablespoons maple syrup |
| 6 | ounces mixed baby bitter greens |
| 4 | ounces blue cheese, crumbled |
| 2 | large firm pears, sliced and tossed in lemon juice |
| ¼ | cup dressing (olive oil and vinegar) |

### Preparation

Heat a skillet; add nuts and maple syrup. Stir for 5 minutes over medium heat to caramelize. Turn out onto a plate for 10 minutes to cool and turn crunchy.

In a mixing bowl, gently combine the washed greens, crumbled blue cheese, and dressing. Arrange on a serving platter in a thin layer. Top with the pear slices and nut halves. Serve immediately. Serves 6.

# Tangier Corn Pudding

### Anne Beckner

Tangier Island lies off the coast of Virginia in Chesapeake Bay. It can only be reached by boat and has a population of less than a thousand. It has changed very little over the years since it was explored and named by John Smith in the mid-1600s. The British used it as a staging area during the war of 1812. Linguists have found the natives interesting because of the old English dialects that have persisted from the time of the founding.

There are a few gift shops, three bed and breakfasts, two or three restaurants, a hardware store, and one pay phone. Fishing, oystering, and crabbing are the main occupations, and tourism flourishes in the summer. There are very few cars, and natives and tourists get around on bikes, mopeds and golf carts. Visitors are encouraged to bring cash because there are no ATMs, but credit cards can be used. It is a great birding area to spot water fowl and to watch the seasonal migrations. The wild marshes and isolated beaches are very peaceful.

I visited Tangier Island with my parents when I was in college, and they returned several times to enjoy the birding and shelling on the quiet beaches. The isolated, marshy island is not conducive to agriculture or cattle raising, so canned goods have been used to create unique recipes. My parents enjoyed sampling the cuisine in the restaurants and found this corn pudding to be simple and delicious. I have made it all my adult life and often make it for pot lucks when side dishes are needed. It goes together quickly when you are pressed for time and are out of fresh vegetables.

# Tangier Corn Pudding

### Ingredients

- 2 tablespoons cornstarch
- ⅓ cup sugar
- 2 eggs
- 1 14-ounce can creamed corn
- 1 14-ounce can evaporated milk

### Preparation

Preheat oven to 350°F. Mix together cornstarch and sugar. Add eggs and blend. Add creamed corn and evaporated milk to mixture.

Pour mixture into a lightly buttered 9x9-inch or similar size casserole dish and bake approximately 1 hour or until a knife inserted comes out clean.

Serves 6.

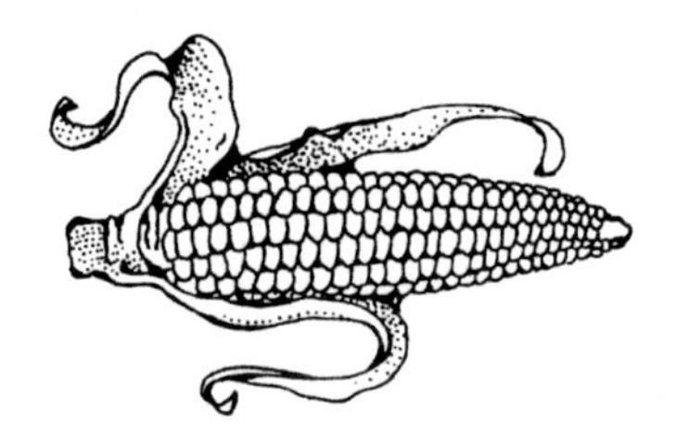

---

**Anne Beckner** has always loved to cook and comes from a long line of good cooks who taught her a lot. The happy result is that her grown children all have a keen interest in good food and cooking. Even her six-year-old grandson has been eating brie and Greek olives since he was an infant. Anne likes to read cookbooks, especially regional ones, and to experiment with new recipes.

# *Rachel Misegades' Catsup*

**Katherine Misegades**

My first shock when I moved into a dorm at college was when I discovered that not all ketchup is created equal—or spelled the same. I have a recipe, Tomato Catsup, on a card that was typed on my mother's 1927 Underwood.

Even now, when I look at that card, I can smell it cooking. For me, it is an August odor. I'd run in from play and the whole house would be perfumed with Mama's ketchup. Sometimes, she'd let me cap the bottles. She reused the glass bottles from year to year, but she bought new caps and had a hand-capping machine that was fun to use. Her ketchup was not only aromatic, it was a bit on the chunky side. It was also so delicious that it was hard to make the batch last until the following August.

Until I went to college, I'd never tasted a commercial brand of ketchup. It paled in comparison to Mama's. In the years since, I've never found a brand that tastes as good.

---

**Katherine Misegades** lives in Fort Wayne, Indiana, and works as a graphic artist. In addition to web design, illustration, and print production, she designs and publishes patterns for hand-knitted garments. Since joining SCN in 2002 as a member of eCircle 12, she became a facilitator for eCircle 14 in 2005.

# *Rachel's Tomato Catsup*

**(Ketchup)**

### Ingredients

| | |
|---|---|
| 1 | bushel tomatoes, quartered |
| 1½ | pints vinegar |
| 3 | cups sugar |
| 2 | teaspoons cloves |
| 1 | teaspoon red pepper |
| 2 | onions, chopped |
| 3½ | tablespoons salt |
| 2 | teaspoons cinnamon |
| 2 | teaspoons allspice |
| 1 | teaspoon black pepper |

### Preparation

Cook tomatoes and drain off the clear liquid (this can be canned for soup). After running the tomatoes through the colander, add the remaining ingredients to 12 pints of the thick puree. Cook slowly until thick. Seal in hot, clean jars.

Makes 6–7 pints.

### Tips and Notes

A bushel is an 8-gallon container. For tomatoes, this will be equivalent to about 24 pounds.

Boil the thick puree until it is reduced by about half.

# *Adventures in an Indian Kitchen: Jackfruit*

**Janice Kvale**

My husband and I lived in Cochin, Kerala, a city in southern India for nearly a year. I took this as an opportunity to learn as much about the country and culture as I could, which included cooking almost exclusively Indian food. This required learning different methods of preparation and new names for familiar foods. I got recipes from Indian cookbooks readily available in local bookstores. I learned the names of ingredients from recognizing the produce in the market and reading labels, where they were available. Okra was sold as ladyfingers, eggplant was *brinjal*, and potatoes were *aloo*. Then there was produce not found in a typical U.S. supermarket, such as jackfruit.

Jackfruit grows on large trees, often coming right off the trunk on a thick stalk. They are quite large and heavy, perhaps one foot by three foot ovals, like giant green eggs. For the rural population, they are free for the picking in the countryside. In more populated areas, I saw hawkers selling jackfruit stacked like cord wood beside the road.

I was determined to explore this strange fruit. One day I saw a pile of jackfruit stacked up outside the farmer's cooperative produce market across the road from our apartment building. Jackfruit may be used green or ripe; frankly I couldn't tell the difference. Since it was early in the season, I assumed the jackfruit was green.

I crossed the busy street careful to dodge the auto-rickshaws and scurried quickly when there was a break in the bus and auto traffic. The manager at the produce market spoke as much English as I did Malayam, which was none at all. I signaled what I wanted and he grabbed his cleaver and looked at me for approval of the amount he thought I should purchase. I was surprised and pleased that I didn't have to purchase the whole thing. I waggled my head, yes, in Indian fashion (side to side instead of forward and backward), carried my prize home, placed it on the kitchen counter and wondered what to do next. My friend, Ajitha, had warned me that if I wanted to prepare jackfruit I would have to grease everything that came in contact with it including my hands, as the juice was very sticky. I grabbed a choice of knives, put on latex gloves, greased the knives and gloves and began.

I found the jackfruit had four separate parts, and I didn't know which was the one to eat. There was a leathery rough green outer skin; logically this would be discarded. Inside there were large brown seeds encased in slippery orange pouches. These were suspended in a white, fibrous infrastructure. I decided the orange pouches were the food and threw out the rest. It took about three tedious hours to dissect my jackfruit. Ripe, the orange pods may be eaten as they are. I found them quite sweet, fleshy, and a bit … well, slimy. The flavor was nice enough, but this may be an acquired taste. It was not like tasting a mango for the first time when I knew instantly it would be my favorite fruit forever! The jackfruit *thoran* (a "dry" dish) I made was pretty good, with a bit of sweetness to the flavor. Then I found a recipe calling for jackfruit seeds, but I had thrown those away.

Later, my friend, Shanti, gave me another piece of ripe jackfruit from the tree in her yard and a lesson in dissection. She showed me how to counter the stickiness by rubbing the inside portions with the cut side of half of a coconut shell. Now I also had jackfruit seeds to use. Like the whole fruit, they required a bit of processing. I quartered them

*Continues on page 46*

# *Jackfruit Thoran*

### Ingredients

| | |
|---|---|
| 2 | 20-ounce cans green jackfruit in brine |
| ½ | teaspoon ground turmeric |
| 1 | cup fresh coconut meat |
| ¼ | teaspoon cumin seeds |
| ½ | teaspoon chili powder |
| 2 | cloves fresh garlic |
| 2 | tablespoons vegetable oil |
| ½ | teaspoon black mustard seeds |
| 1–2 | dry red chilies, broken in half |
| 10–20 | curry leaves |
| 1 | teaspoon salt or to taste |

### Preparation

Drain the canned jackfruit. Chunk the jackfruit pieces into smaller sizes for processing in a food processor or blender and pulse until shredded. Pour jackfruit into a large mixing bowl. Mix in turmeric. Set aside.

Put the coconut into the food processor with the cumin seeds, chili powder, and coarsely chopped garlic. Pulse until ground together. Add to the jackfruit and mix.

In a large frying pan, heat the vegetable oil until shimmering but not smoking. Sauté the mustard seeds, dry red chilis, and curry leaves until brown. This takes no more than 30 seconds. Add the jackfruit mixture and salt, and sauté together until the mixture is dry. Serve hot as a side or main dish.

Serves 6.

### Tips and Notes

Canned jackfruit comes in brine or syrup. Use the brine for cooking. I have not experimented with frozen jackfruit. My Indian grocer tells me jackfruit is now being grown near the Mexican border but is very expensive.

Avoid dried, sweetened coconut. Frozen grated coconut is available, if you do not want to spend time processing a fresh coconut.

Grown in Florida, fresh curry leaves may also be available at the Indian grocery.

---

In 2003, **Janice Kvale** received a U.S. State Department Fulbright Award to live and teach in India. She was located in Cochin, Kerala, a seacoast city in southwest India, where she took advantage of the time to experiment with Indian cuisine using locally available ingredients. Janice says she was fortunate to have Indian friends to guide her in her kitchen adventures.

*Continued from page 44*

and peeled off a tough brown skin revealing a starchy white interior. The part inside took about an hour of boiling in turmeric water (nearly all dishes in India get turmeric, which I learned is more for antiseptic purposes than seasoning!) to get tender. The recipe called for mashing the seeds, but they were too firm to mash with the potato masher. I got out the grinder, a heavy-duty version of a food processor unique to India, and whipped those seeds into a large clot. The clot was tossed into a soupy *brinjal* (eggplant) curry and functioned to thicken it nicely. It was pretty good, though it nearly blew our heads off even after I cut the suggested number of fresh green chilies in half. I guess I shouldn't have used all twelve of the dried red chilies in addition to the four little green ones.

# *Potato Girl*

**Janan Hale**

"One of these days you're going to turn into a potato," my grandmother said to me more than once. Being a scrawny five year old I thought a lot about that. I wasn't sure if she was kidding me. Her voice sounded certain about the possible outcome of too many potatoes and she wasn't the joking type. Mom and I lived with my paternal grandparents while my daddy worked in a shipyard during the war. He came home on weekends.

The kitchen was a small room. The table would accommodate three or four people and was used for a breakfast or a quick lunch setting. I remember sitting there watching my Irish grandmother busy herself with something tasty. Her flour could be sifted directly into a bowl from a cabinet she called her pie safe. The dash churn was a step away on the screened in porch. That's where Mema taught me how to make butter by agitating the plunger up and down in the cold cows milk. There were usually fresh-from-the-garden vegetables in baskets. The dining room, with a round oak table and a big buffet, was just off the kitchen. To walk into that room was a reminder of festivities with laughter, delicious smells, family and great food, usually including potatoes.

With the large garden for fruits and vegetables in season, the bountiful pecan tree shading the back of the

---

**Janan Hale** has lived most of her life in East Texas where she graduated from Stephen F. Austin State University with a degree in Elementary Education. For the last five years Janan has looked forward to joining with friends to write and discuss writing with the Memory Keepers story circle in Tyler, Texas. Art is another one of her interests and she loves spending time with any one of her ten grandchildren.

house, chickens and cows just behind the shed, and a grandmother who was masterful in her culinary skills, we were well prepared should there be an emergency. In a wartime setting when our small town practiced air raid warnings at night, I never felt secure. We would sit close together in a small, inside bedroom with a heavy blanket over the window, listening to a radio and awaiting the siren sound that announced all clear. I was told we would probably never need to hide from any danger; it was just a drill for preparedness.

Maybe war-time fears affected my appetite. Despite the abundance of food, I was never very hungry. That is why my Mema whipped up mashed potatoes with fresh milk and butter, knowing I would need no enticement for that. Potatoes, baked, scalloped, in soup, or fixed most any way, were my comfort foods. They still are.

# Potato Casserole

### Ingredients

| | |
|---|---|
| 1 | 30-ounce bag of frozen shredded hash brown potatoes |
| 1 | stick butter (4 ounces) |
| 1 | 10-ounce can undiluted cream of chicken soup |
| 8 | ounces sour cream |
| 8 | ounces grated Cheddar cheese |
| | Crushed cornflakes or seasoned breadcrumbs |

### Preparation

Preheat the oven to 350°F.

Butter a 13x9-inch Pyrex dish. Mix melted butter with soup and sour cream in a large bowl. Add half the grated cheese. Stir in the hash brown potatoes.

Pour into the buttered baking dish. Top with cornflakes or breadcrumbs and the remaining cheese. Bake the casserole at 350°F. until it is bubbly, about 30 minutes.

Serves 8–10.

### Tips and Notes

Country style frozen shredded hash brown potatoes work well in this recipe.

You can make this recipe with fresh shredded or grated potato, but you may need to increase the baking time.

# *No More Parsnips*

**Bee Jay Gwennap**

Times were tough during the Great Depression of 1929–39. The fertile field behind our house in Bernards Township, New Jersey, was tilled and planted and provided an abundance of fruits and vegetables for us during those years. It contained not just the luscious tomatoes for which New Jersey is justly famed but everything from carrots and potatoes to broccoli and beets. A variety of lettuces, cabbages, and cucumbers were turned into tasty salads. We even had our own apple and peach trees, broad rows of strawberries, and currants and crab apples for making jelly. The one crop missing in our garden was parsnips.

The Parsnip Story took place before I was born, but I know it well enough from its constant telling. It was the beginning of the Depression and my newly married parents, Betty and George, were living in a vacant farmhouse with lots of love but little money. With only two dollars left for food, George was sent out to shop. He returned with a bushel of parsnips. My mother, who would never be known as an outstanding cook, racked her brain for ways to fix them. She boiled them, baked them, stewed them, and fried them. Finally the basket was empty and she adopted a new law that she adhered to for the rest of her ninety-eight years: *No more parsnips.*

That was the reason I grew up knowing the euphoric smell of Chicken Fricassee when I entered the back kitchen door, snitching pieces of Cheddar from the cutting board as she assembled her Macaroni and Cheese Casserole, and finishing meals with a fragrant Apple Brown Betty made from the scraps of stale bread, but I never tasted a single parsnip. Depression meals tended to be repetitious and heavy on the carbohydrates, but they could be delicious.

I respected the *No more parsnips* rule until years later when I finally learned to appreciate this humble, pale, and hairy root product, introduced to it by my daughters Gayle and Ellen. Their recipes come not from some grease-spotted cookbook or tattered index card but from the computer. A few clicks of the keys and they are borrowing recipes from Martha, Emeril, or *Cooking Light*. Modern cooking has broken the family curse on the parsnip and I include this pungent vegetable in many of the dishes that I cook, like my roasted root vegetables.

---

Born and raised in Basking Ridge, New Jersey, **Bee Jay Gwennap** has also called Pennsylvania, West Virginia, and North Carolina home. A graduate of West Virginia Wesleyan College, she was Home Economist for Columbia Gas Company. Two daughters, four grandchildren, and an interest in the arts have also kept her occupied. Watercolor painting and writing poetry are two of her current favorite activities.

# Roasted Root Vegetables

### Ingredients

6 cups mixed parsnips, carrots, and turnips, cut into chunks
2 onions, cut in wedges
2 tablespoons olive oil
1 tablespoon brown sugar
1 teaspoon salt
1 tablespoon balsamic vinegar
Chopped parsley

### Preparation

Preheat the oven to 450°F.

Toss parsnip, carrot, and turnip chunks with onions wedges and olive oil. Place on an oiled cookie sheet and sprinkle with brown sugar and salt.

Bake at 450°F. for 1 hour, turning everything over with a spatula after 30 minutes. Sprinkle with balsamic vinegar and add some chopped parsley before you serve.

Serves 6–8.

---

# Lean Times

### A Writing Prompt

For our parents' generation, times of plenty were often interspersed with times of food scarcity. We may have experienced this ourselves as we grew up, or we may have just heard about the lean times from our parents and grandparents. What are some of the stories your family shares of lean times and the foods that the family had to rely on (perhaps more than they would have wished) to get through? Write down one of these stories.

# *Grandma Franklin's Pickled Eggs*

**Susan Wittig Albert**

My mother grew up in western Missouri, on a small farm in Polk Township, Sullivan County, and when my brother John and I were small, during the Second World War, we'd go to visit there on the train. "Going down home," Mother called it. The farm is gone now, but I still think of it as "down home."

Arriving was always an exciting affair. Uncle Allen would meet us with his '34 Ford at the Trenton railroad station and take us to Milan, where Grandpa met us with his pair of heavy brown farm horses, their hoofs as big as buckets, and the farm wagon. I'd jump into the wagon and climb up on the seat beside Grandpa, so I could admire the deft way he handled those horses and smell their horsy smell, and see the sweat gleaming on their smooth flanks. And so we would ride to the farm, seven miles away, down a steep hill that required Grandpa to brake the wagon wheels and say soft words to the horses, then up another hill, even steeper. Grandpa would lift the leather reins and chirp encouragement between his teeth, and the horses would prick their ears and pull with a good will, and I would cling to the edge of the seat and hold my breath and wonder if we would make it. We always did.

Grandpa had a pair of milk cows in the pasture, and each cow had a calf (oh, those brown calves, with new brown coats and white faces and wondering eyes). We had fresh milk all summer long. I milked my first cow in the pre-dawn light the summer I was seven and drank her milk proudly at the breakfast table that very morning. There were pigs for hams and bacon, huge, blundering, black-and-white creatures that spent their days lazing in the mud of their pens. I was fond of them and felt grown-up as I took them their slop: a heavy bucket of leftovers from the table and the tops and leaves from the garden vegetables and milk that had "gone off." Early on, I made the connection between the pigs in the pen and the bacon and ham on the table and felt grateful to them for sharing themselves with us. And share they did, generously. Grandma served those hams in thick slices, fried, with red-eye gravy, and we had bacon for breakfast, with fresh eggs and thick, flaky biscuits.

Grandma had a garden, with beans and peas and potatoes and tomatoes and lovely sweet corn. And she had chickens—a couple of dozen laying hens for eggs, and their rooster, and always young chickens for frying. The rooster was a glory, with sweeping feathers, red and gold and iridescent in the sun, and a ruby red comb and yellow legs and gleaming spurs. The hens, his harem, flocked eagerly when he found a grasshopper and clucked to them: "Come, my pretties, and see what I have found for you. Come, lovely ladies, ladies mine."

And the eggs, yes, the eggs, all of them speckled brown, with large orange yolks the color of sunset. It was my job to gather them, fresh-laid and warm, and I learned not to mind the hens' sharp beaks, always ready to peck my hand

---

**Susan Wittig Albert** is the best-selling author of three popular mystery series. Her book, *Writing from Life: Telling Your Soul's Story*, was the impetus for the Story Circle Network, which she founded in 1997. She has three children, eight grandchildren, and a great-grandson. She and her husband Bill live in the Texas Hill Country, where she enjoys gardening, textile and fiber crafts, and reading.

when I reached under their soft feathers to pull out the eggs. We took them as soon as they were laid, Grandma explained, because if we waited, the bull snakes would come and take them first. "I ain't spendin' good money on chicken corn so them snakes can eat eggs," she'd say huffily.

We ate lots of eggs and I liked them any way Grandma fixed them. But my favorite was her pickled eggs. When the youngest hens first began to lay, their eggs were smaller, and Grandma prized them, because little eggs were prettier, pickled, than big eggs. A plate of pickled eggs always dressed up the Sunday dinner table, she said. Fascinated by the pink color and tangy taste, I loved to help her make them, but when it came time to eat, it was rare that I got more than half an egg. Sunday dinners on the Franklin farm were well-attended, and the men folks ate before the women and children. Grandma's pickled eggs were almost all gone by the time I got to the table.

I found Grandma's handwritten recipe not long ago, stuck between the pages of the *Pure Food Cook Book*, which was compiled by the Farm Women of Missouri in 1945—my mother's standby cookbook and recipe file. Here it is, in case your hens are starting to lay. If not, you can buy small eggs at the grocery store, and if you don't happen to have your own home-canned beets, store-bought will do as well.

# Pickled Pink Eggs

### Ingredients

| | |
|---|---|
| 1 | dozen small eggs |
| 1 | pint small beets (not pickled) |
| 2 | cups cider vinegar |
| 3 | small onions sliced |
| 1 | teaspoon salt |
| 1 | teaspoon sugar |
| ½ | teaspoon pickling spices |

### Preparation

Hard boil the eggs and peel them. Push a fork into the middle of each egg. Put the eggs in a deep crock. In a pan, heat the beets, vinegar, onions, salt, sugar, and spices until just ready to boil. Cool for 10 minutes. Pour over eggs. Put a plate on top and put in the refrigerator for at least a week.

Remove eggs from the brine and slice in half. Serve on a pretty glass dish, garnished with fresh parsley or mint.

Makes 12 eggs.

# *The Chicken or the Egg*

**Marian Haigh**

Grandma and Grandpa's farm was a natural classroom. To roam all day through the woods and play under the big oak trees on the rocky ledge or run around with the dogs, check out the chickens and cows, or pick pecans from your very own tree gave a range of experiences not found in school books. Even the sagging, unpainted farm buildings clustered around the house were of interest to the inquiring mind. The buildings included a new cinderblock dairy barn, the old stone barn, the old chicken house, the sometimes chicken house, a tool shed, the cool, dark cellar (scary), and the outhouse (really scary at night).

Grandma's chicken house was an old wooden building with a low roof and a series of windows on one side that allowed the sun to drift through the dust and little feathers that wafted in the air. The nesting boxes ranged along the wall opposite the windows. It was a test of will to gather eggs. Bunny usually stood outside the door of the chicken house for a few moments to become mentally prepared when she was by herself. Grandma Rose had explained how to slowly slide your hand under the chicken's warm breast, gently clutch the egg, and carefully draw it out. But the chickens had a sixth sense about small, nervous intruders, and their chicken grumbles could easily accelerate to loud clacking and swift pecks on little hands. Grandma usually gathered the eggs from the grumpy, broody hens.

One morning playing hide-and-seek, Bunny quickly ducked into the chicken house to hide and startled a laying hen. The chicken cackled loudly as she rose up from her nest, flapping her wings, and an egg pooped out of her rear end! It was an astonishing sight and it was hard to say who was more surprised. Bunny turned and ran pell-mell into the house, found Grandma, and breathlessly related her amazing discovery that chicken eggs came out of a chicken's behind! But Grandma took the information in stride as she had already known about it for some time. She explained that eggs were made inside the chicken's body from the food they ate and had to come out somewhere.

The next time Grandma made homemade egg noodles she called Bunny into the kitchen to add to the egg lesson. Rose had killed and dressed a hen for Sunday lunch and true to her frugal nature was using the hen's inside, unformed eggs to make the noodles. She held the little eggs in her hands for Bunny to see. They were like a coil of beads strung together, little yellow balls, so new the whites had not yet formed. The largest egg was the size of a shooter marble and each globe next to it was successively smaller until the smallest egg was the size of a little green pea. The strand of eggs lay in a spiral like one half of a large pearl necklace and was a marvel to behold. Grandma worked the little eggs with a fork into her flour until it formed a stiff dough. Then she kneaded it and rolled it out on the wood tabletop into a thin, uneven circle and began to slice noodle strips with a knife. The deep yellow yolks lent their color to the dough. When cooked, the noodles would be slightly chewy and have a subtle, wonderful egg flavor.

The farm gave a child many ideas to examine and where else could you see so clearly an example of that old brain teaser, "Which came first, the chicken or the egg?"

# Rich Egg Noodles

### Ingredients

- 2 cups all purpose flour
- ½ cup cake flour
- ½ teaspoon salt (plus a pinch or two)
- 4 large egg yolks
- 3 large eggs
- 1 teaspoon extra virgin olive oil
- Semolina (pasta flour) for working the dough

### Preparation

Combine the dry ingredients and pulse in the food processor to mix. In a small bowl, mix the eggs and olive oil together. With the food processor running, add the eggs and the olive oil slowly through the feed tube until the dough forms a ball on top of the blades. You may not need all the egg mixture or you might have to add another egg yolk depending on your flour.

Gather up the dough and divide it into two portions and form them into balls. Dust your counter or table with semolina flour and knead the ball on the flour until smooth, approximately 3 minutes. Repeat with the second ball of dough. Wrap each ball tightly in plastic wrap and refrigerate the dough about 1½ to 2 hours to chill. Chilling the dough makes it easier to roll out.

Again spread semolina flour on the work surface and roll the ball of dough. Roll and flip and roll and flip the dough, adding more semolina if necessary, until it is about 1/16 inch thick. Or roll it thinner, if you can. Tip: after I have rolled the dough to about ⅛ inch thick I let it rest for about 5 or 10 minutes so it can dry out a bit. Then rolling it thinner is easier.

Use a sharp knife and cut the noodles in thin strips and gather them loosely on a tray making sure they don't clump together. You can also cut squares of dough to make ravioli.

Bring a large pan of water to boil and slide the noodles in. You can add salt and olive oil to the water if you wish. Check the noodles for doneness and drain when they are ready.

Serves 4.

### Tips and Notes

This dough freezes wonderfully—but thaw the frozen dough in the refrigerator, not on the counter, because of the fresh eggs.

You don't have to have a pasta machine—just roll it out on the counter and cut it into strips like Grandma! It's easy.

---

**Marian Haigh** was born in Pittsburg, Kansas, in 1951 and grew up in very small towns in a rural setting. She received a B.F.A. from Arkansas State University in 1973. Since then she has worked in her studio, hand building ceramic vessels, teaching workshops, and exhibiting locally and nationally. Marian lives with her husband and a very bad cat in Austin, Texas. They divide their time between the city and a cabin in the Texas Hill Country.

# *Tips on Making and Cooking Pierogi*

## *(and Why I Won't Be Doing It)*

**Linda C. Wisniewski**

On the first pages of my mother's well-worn cookbook are five recipes for pierogi dough. The differences between them are tiny: one egg or two; a quarter or a half cup of water; one and three-fourths or two cups of flour; lukewarm water or water, lukewarm. And those are just the ingredients. When I get to the directions I am charmed by the English-as-a-Second-Language phrasing. The book has no publication date, but the authors are likely Polish immigrants. The pages are yellowed and brittle. The paper cover is mended with masking tape. Alongside many of the recipes, my mother's careful handwriting: "Delicious" or "Make in white Teflon pan" or "This cake is OK if apples are very *thinly* sliced." She drew a big X through that recipe, probably deciding it wasn't worth another try.

Mom died in 2003 and I've kept her cookbook only for sentimental reasons. I won't be making my own pierogi. The directions are complicated and time-consuming. Talk about "slow food!" Still, I think I know why there are five different pierogi recipes, plus "tips" and even more recipes for fillings.

Pierogi are a national dish, the Polish version of ravioli. They remind us of our *babcis* (grandmas) and Polish Americans still eat them on holidays. To Polish ladies of a certain age, pierogi were a point of pride. If I go back in my mind to my childhood, I can hear them argue whether or not to add milk to the dough, how long to "rest the dough, covered," and whether it's better to fry them or "pour slightly browned butter over the pierogi." These instructions are included in the book published by the Felician Sisters, a Polish order of nuns who taught at the grade school that I went to and my mother before me, and though they scared me as a girl, holding their book warms my heart.

Before I even get to the recipes, there is an introductory page of tips on making and cooking pierogi: "Dough…must always be soft and well-kneaded. Knead dough till smooth and well-blended. Hard dough makes tough pierogi….(*I'm scared already; they'll say I make it too hard!*) Always rest dough at least fifteen minutes…Dry dough will not seal well. Always keep your dough covered….(*Mom taught me to put a clean dishtowel over the bowl.)* Place a small spoonful of filling a little to one side on each round of dough….Drop pierogi into salted boiling water (but 'a full rollicking boil will make the pierogi fall apart.' *How do you know it's rollicking before it is?*) Mix lightly with wooden spoon….Lift out of water with a perforated spoon….(*I don't have a wooden* or *a perforated spoon!*) Never crowd or pile pierogi. The uncooked will stick and cooked will loose (sic) shape and lightness…." *Whew! I'm tired just reading this.*

My ancestry is Polish and so is my husband Steve's. We like our little stuffed dough rounds fried in melted

---

**Linda C. Wisniewski** is a part-time substitute librarian in Bucks County, Pennsylvania, where she writes for a weekly newspaper and teaches memoir classes at Bucks County Community College. Her work has been published in the *Christian Science Monitor*, the *Philadelphia Inquirer*, the *Rose and Thorn*, *Out of Line*, *Mindprints*, and other regional and literary journals. She was nominated for a Pushcart Prize. Linda's memoir, *Off Kilter*, is forthcoming in 2008 from Pearlsong Press.

## *Pierogi*

### Dough Ingredients

| | |
|---|---|
| 2 | cups sifted flour |
| 1 | egg |
| 2 | tablespoons melted butter |
| ½ | cup lukewarm water |
| 3 | tablespoons sour cream |
| 3 | tablespoons vegetable oil |
| | Pinch of salt |

### Preparation

Mix all ingredients together lightly and knead in bowl. Rest it for ½ hour, covered. Then knead the dough on a floured board and roll out to ⅛ inch thickness.

Cut out circles with a cup, glass, or doughnut cutter (remove center cutter from the doughnut cutter.) Fill with favorite filling, pressing edges well together, like for turnovers. Bring water to a boil and add salt like for cooking noodles. Drop the pierogi gently into the boiling water. When the pierogi come to the top, cut down heat to a slow boil. (Full rollicking boil will make the pierogi fall apart.) Boil for about 10 minutes and take out with slotted spoon into colander placed in a small pan or pot. Rinse very lightly, with cold water, drain and place on serving plate. Pour slightly browned butter over the pierogi.

### Ingredients

| | |
|---|---|
| 1 | head cabbage |
| 1 | 1-pound can or package sauerkraut |
| 1 | large onion |
| 4 | ounces butter |

### Preparation

Rinse sauerkraut and parboil. Drain. Add shredded cabbage and boil until tender about 15–20 minutes. Drain and cool. Sauté one large onion, chopped, in 1 stick of butter until brown in large skillet. Put cabbage–sauerkraut through grinder. Drain well from most of the water. Add to the sautéed onion and sauté in low heat until flavor blends, 15–20 minutes. Salt and pepper to taste. This also can be done same way with just sauerkraut, or with just cabbage alone. Cool completely before using. Make the filling a day before using.

Makes about 4-dozen pierogi.

---

butter but we buy them at the Polish grocery on holidays.

My ethnicity is not wrapped up in my cooking skills. When I turned sixty, I knew I'd have to let some things go. I wasn't going to accomplish everything I'd attempted, and it was time to stop worrying about it. I will never climb high mountains. Spelunking is out. I gave up practicing the piano and knitting sweaters. I will never learn to knit socks. And I will never mix, knead, cover, cut out, fill, press, seal, boil, lift, drain, rinse and cool pierogi. Writing about it will have to do.

I honor the strong, hard-working women who made the dough and preserved the recipes. There is comfort just remembering how solid, how true, how reliable they were. And I know there is more to their stories. I am grateful for these women who fed their families well, taught their daughters to cook, and gave me the strength to make choices. Just look at page 9: you can have cabbage or sauerkraut filling, potato or cream cheese, prune or apple....Who knew?

# The Joy of Being Thrown Together

**Pat LaPointe**

This "tradition" began as the result of some of my unsuccessful early attempts to multitask. I was in a doctoral program, working part time, trying to keep up with my hormonally driven four daughters, and finding ways to not feel so guilty for not spending time with them. Soon after I began the program, I realized that every week at least one of my responsibilities would not be fulfilled. Sometimes the wash would not be done, sometimes a chapter would go unread, and sometimes there would be an "all-nighter" in order to keep up. However, most often it was either a grocery list left lying in the bottom of my briefcase or one that was never written resulting in partially empty cabinets, pantries, freezers, and refrigerators.

It always seemed that we eked by during the week, but by Sunday dinner there were slim pickin's. As dinner hour approached, there would come a knock on the door of my study. "Mom, what's for dinner?" would come the call.

My usual response was, "Oh, *#@**! I didn't get to the grocery store."

Fearing having starving children and dealing with the resulting guilt, I would race to the kitchen and begin to throw open the doors to the freezer, cabinets, and pantry. Thus began my now infamous "throw-together dinners." It was amazing what you could do with a pound of frozen meat, some noodles, sauce of any kind, and several varieties of canned veggies.

It wasn't long before my daughters realized that Sunday dinners would be mysterious and indescribable until the results of the "throw-together" was on their plates. Then something strange happened. They not only began to want to eat the throw-together meals but also to participate in their preparation. Now, instead of panicking and feeling inadequate as a mother, I had four young women flinging open the cabinets, pantry, freezer, and fridge. Some of their suggestions for combinations of ingredients had us laughing so hard that at least one of us made a mad dash to the nearest bathroom. There were the beans, corn, and tomato sauce dishes when a week had gone by without stocking the freezer with meat. There were the "mostly meat" with sauce and noodles dishes when the cupboards and pantry were bare. No two dinners were ever alike and to this day have ever been repeated.

I came to really enjoy putting away the books long enough to spend time with my throw-together chefs. I have long forgotten what it was I was studying on any given Sunday but I'll treasure the memories of time spent with my girls.

---

**Pat LaPointe** is the Director of WomensVoices: An Enrichment Center for Midlife Women, located in Prospect Heights, Illinois, which offers workshops on topics of interest to midlife women. She has published essays and articles addressing women's midlife issues and is currently collecting survey data that examines the past and present experiences, future goals, and wisdom gained by women age fifty to sixty-five.

# *Where's-the-Meat? Pasta–Bean Medley*

**Ingredients**

| | |
|---|---|
| 1 | 15-ounce can kidney or black beans |
| 1 | 15-ounce can corn |
| 2 | 15-ounce can either stewed or seasoned diced tomatoes |
| 1 | 8-ounce package elbow noodles |
| | Garlic salt/powder, as desired |
| | Onion salt/powder, as desired |
| | Chili powder (if you want a Mexican dish) |
| | Pizza seasoning (if you want an Italian dish) |

**Preparation**

Cook noodles according to the package directions. While the noodles are boiling, heat beans, corn, tomatoes, and dry ingredients. Drain the cooked noodles and add to the bean, corn, and sauce mixture. Serve.

Serves 5.

**Tips and Notes**

Goes great with corn muffins or buttermilk biscuits—if you remembered to buy them!

Optional: Add 2 cups of shredded Cheddar or mozzarella cheese to the mixture and microwave for 2–3 minutes before serving.

# The Scents of Oklahoma Rain

**Matilda Butler**

It's almost noon when I look up from my math lesson. A glance out the window confirms what I had guessed—what I had smelled. Across the playing fields of Linwood Elementary School, I see the dark Oklahoma storm clouds racing toward us. The rain is coming; the rain is coming.

The first large raindrops splash on the windowsill. Miss Lightfoot dashes to close the classroom window, her thick low-heeled black shoes clomping on the wooden floor. I had smelled the rain coming—willing it to come. For me, rain means a special chili dinner.

Today, almost six decades later, I watch rain falling gently outside my study. Suddenly I smell chili, garlic, cumin, oregano, and onion in the air, although I haven't even started cooking dinner. If the years weren't enough of a separation from these childhood scents, there is also distance, fifteen hundred miles. I now live in Silicon Valley where the land yields computer chips rather than Oklahoma City where the land yields oil from under the state capitol itself! Do I still have time today to start a batch of chili?

Rain, especially winter rain in my childhood, brought the likelihood that we would enjoy a spicy, fragrant chili either at El Charrito or at home. A meal out was a rare treat when I was growing up in the '50s. The rain-borne expectation of a restaurant meal was enchanting. Looking back, I realize that El Charrito was doubly unusual. First, it was housed in an Art Deco building in the Paseo District that eventually became an Oklahoma City landmark, an unlikely exterior for a Mexican restaurant. Second, the owners were helping to create one of America's most authentic fusion cuisines—Tex-Mex. Maria Cuellar Alvarado, born in Texas, and her husband Luis Alvarado, born in Mexico, brought together their favorite recipes and unique spices from both sides of the border to develop distinctive dishes for the family restaurant they opened in the late 1930s.

I fondly remember one evening in about 1953 when my father asked the purpose of a sign-up sheet on a battered clipboard next to the cash register.

Luis Alvarado told him, "When I left my small village in Mexico, I swore to all my friends that I would not return until I could come back with a fleet of Cadillacs. They laughed at me. Now, I'm taking some of my customers on an auto tour of Mexico. We will make many stops and eat wonderful food. But you can only sign up if you drive a Cadillac. I will enter my village at the head of a long procession of Cadillacs."

My father was intrigued and always willing to test the limits. He responded, "I have a good friend who would

*Continues on page 60*

---

**Matilda Butler** graduated magna cum laude from Boston University, earned an M.A. from Stanford University and a Ph.D. from Northwestern University. Butler is listed in Who's Who of American Women. An author, psychologist, and entrepreneur, she currently teaches at the University of California–Santa Cruz, Gavilan College, and privately. Her collective memoir, *Rosie's Daughters: The "First Woman To" Generation Tells Its Story,* will be published in 2007. Further information is available at her website, www.WomensMemoirs.com.

# Matilda's Vegan Oklahoma Chili

## Ingredients

- 3 cups large sized Textured Vegetable Protein (TVP)
- 3 tablespoons soy sauce
- 2 tablespoons liquid smoke
- Boiling water to cover
- 2 large onions, chopped
- 3 tablespoons olive oil
- 3–5 garlic cloves, minced
- 1 tablespoon cumin
- 3 tablespoons chili powder
- 1 teaspoon chili flakes
- 2 heaping teaspoons dried oregano
- 2 tablespoons Masa Harina or corn flour
- 1 jar Classico spaghetti sauce
- 1 15-ounce can tomato sauce
- 1 15-ounce can Muir Glen organic pizza sauce
- 1 14-ounce can Muir Glen fire-roasted diced tomatoes or fresh-style diced tomatoes
- 4 cups cooked pinto beans and broth
- 4 cups cooked black beans
- Salt to taste
- 3 tablespoons unsweetened cocoa powder (optional)
- Chopped cilantro and finely chopped sweet or red onion

## Preparation

Prepare the TVP by moistening it with the soy sauce, liquid smoke, and boiling water. Let it sit about 30 minutes, adding more boiling water if necessary to keep the "meat" submerged.

Cook onions in olive oil in a large soup pan. When softened, add garlic and cook for 5 minutes. Add the cumin, chili powder, chili flakes, and oregano, and stir well. Then add Masa Harina or corn flour and stir again. Add spaghetti sauce, tomato sauce, pizza sauce, and the canned tomatoes.

Add the TVP and 8 cups of beans without their cooking broth. Reserve the broth. Stir well and let cook, adding bean broth as needed for consistency. Cook for 15–30 minutes, stirring occasionally. This will reduce the amount of liquid and intensify the flavors. Add salt, if needed, and cocoa powder, if desired.

Serve with chopped cilantro and onion on top.

Serves 16–20.

### Tips and Notes

The recipe makes a lot and it freezes well.

To give the spices time to permeate the dish and harmonize, refrigerate the chili for at least a day.

As a shortcut, use canned beans.

If you like a dark chili, add 3 tablespoons cocoa powder when you add the salt, and stir until absorbed.

*Continued from page 58*

like to go, but he drives a Mercedes. Can he sign up?"

"No," said Alvarado, "only if he drives a Cadillac."

My father, a farm boy and villager himself, liked to tell that story over and over.

Meanwhile, my mother was perfecting her chili. The Depression made her forever economical in her grocery purchases, so a cheap chuck roast, coarsely ground by the butcher, was a favorite starting point for the chili recipe. When the beef was well rendered in the cast iron skillet, my mother began to add the tomatoes and seasoning. She always soaked and cooked her own pinto beans, which became the final ingredient. When I married in 1962, she gave me her chili recipe in a small set of recipe cards saying, "These will help you entertain well and cheaply." Later, she alternated her own recipe with Lady Bird Johnson's Pedernales River Chili. Now I've computerized all my recipes, but I still love handling Mother's handwritten recipe cards.

Fifteen years ago, in an unexpected twist, I became a vegan. Imagine a rare-beef-eating Oklahoman becoming a vegan. At first I thought I'd have to give up a large number of my favorite childhood dishes. Over time, I've found great pleasure in veganizing those recipes, including Mother's chili. Just as Mother once taught me, chili is again a convivial meal in our household. What can be more satisfying on a rainy day than filling the kitchen with the scents of chili, garlic, cumin, oregano, and onion?

"Matilda. … Matilda."

My food reverie vanishes. "Yes, Miss Lightfoot?"

"Will you please pick up the papers and bring them to my desk? Then everyone is released for lunch. Please stay inside today. It's raining."

El Charrito tonight—and Maria always treats me to a little scoop of vanilla ice cream after the chili.

---

# *The Taste of a Place*

**A Writing Prompt**

Often our memories of certain foods are strongly tied to a place, perhaps to our childhood home place or to a place we visited that made a strong impression on us. Remember a favorite food that you first experienced in a special place and that has stayed alive and vivid in your memory. Remember the sights, sounds, smells, and tastes of that special place and special food. Write the story of that place and the food that you associate with it.

# Poultry and Seafood

# *Grandmother's Fried Chicken*

**Pat Flathouse**

My grandmother made the best crispy fried chicken, velvety smooth mashed potatoes, and thick cream gravy that I have ever tasted—makes my mouth water just thinking about it! Grandmother's meal planning began in her back yard, where she kept the hens that laid eggs for the family. I can picture her marching out the kitchen door into the chicken yard and grabbing a plump hen by the feet. In a deft maneuver, she popped its neck and left it to run circles around the back yard until it dropped. Next, the hen went into a pot of boiling hot water on the back porch. The smell was awful, but soon the wet feathers were plucked off and set aside to dry for a pillow-in-the-making.

Grandmother then gutted the chicken and cut it into pieces. She coated each piece on a big cutting board covered with flour, a pinch of salt, and a shake of pepper. Meanwhile, a big cast-iron Dutch oven on Grandmother's stove was heating up the oil to cook the chicken. I believe Grandmother used Crisco to fry her chicken—and for lots of other recipes in her kitchen. She might also have added some of the bacon drippings that she kept in a metal container on the back of her stove.

After Grandmother had the chicken pieces well covered in flour, she carefully lowered them into the popping hot grease in her Dutch oven. The pieces were cooked and turned until they became a crispy golden brown. Meanwhile, Irish potatoes that had been boiled were mashed with big pieces of butter, a dash of milk, a pinch of salt, and a little pepper. Grandmother mashed them with her electric mixer until nary a lump could be found.

When the chicken was done, Grandmother took the pan, threw flour into the leftover oil, and began adding milk, as she stirred it over a low flame. Small crunchy bits left over from the fried chicken were stirred into the mixture, and it all became wonderful cream gravy to be spread over the mashed potatoes.

Somewhere along the line, Grandmother had time to slice tomatoes from her garden and warm up some of her home-canned green beans. All of this made up a delicious meal on a warm summer's evening in West Texas—without air conditioning!

---

**Pat Flathouse's** professional background includes a career of teaching and counseling. She is the author (with Susan Wittig Albert and Catherine Cogburn) of *Your Life, Your Story,* a book designed to help women write their stories. Pat is also a genealogist. She wrote the book, *A Priceless Legacy*, to help women write the stories of their family history. She also teaches workshops on stress management and enjoys traveling and playing with her grandchildren.

# Fried Chicken

### Ingredients

1 young frying chicken
1 cup flour
Salt and pepper to taste
Crisco and bacon drippings

### Preparation

Cut the chicken into serving pieces. Wash the pieces and dry to prevent spattering when they are placed in hot fat. Coat each piece in flour. Then, salt and pepper each piece.

Heat enough fat in a deep cast-iron skillet to have a ½–¾-inch layer. Brown chicken pieces lightly in hot fat, then reduce the heat, and cover the skillet.

Cook slowly until tender, 30 minutes to 1 hour, depending on the size of the chicken. Accompany the fried chicken with cream gravy, if desired.

Serves 4.

### Tips and Notes

You may substitute fat or lard for the Crisco and bacon drippings.

# Cream Gravy

### Ingredients

4 tablespoons fat from fried chicken
4 tablespoons flour
2 cups milk
Salt and pepper to taste

### Preparation

Remove the cooked chicken from the pan and keep warm. Drain off all but 4 tablespoons of fat. Add 4 tablespoons of flour and cook until brown. Add 2 cups of milk and cook about 5 minutes or until thickened. Stir in the brown bits that cling to the pan. Season the gravy with salt and pepper. Serve hot with fried chicken and mashed potatoes.

# Chicken and Dumplings

**Theresa May**

Long before I was born, every dinnertime in Grandma Morton's kitchen was a tableau of rowdy weather-hardened men, hungry from the fields, and a bustle of daughters, their faces pink with heat, helping. Those girls were no slouches at the stove, but none of them would ever top Grandma's gift. I was eighteen when she died, but right up to the end, whatever she served at her table smelled like baking day in paradise and tasted twice as good.

Grandma lived in her later years with her youngest daughter, Golda Bertha (Snook, to anybody who really knew her), and Golda's husband, Dudley Ivey. Not far from their house, plopped down in the middle of West Texas cotton fields, were carefully tended fruit trees and a truck patch lush with seasonal vegetables and melons. While I loved the platters of fried okra and corn on the cob and fresh tomatoes still warm and velvety-smelling from the garden, and the peach cobblers and fruit preserves that were laid out for every meal, my favorite dish—the one I begged Grandma to fix when she visited us in our nearby town or we visited her on the farm—was chicken-and-dumplings. She was the queen of dumplings—"slicks," she called hers—and didn't have much patience for the biscuity lumps lesser cooks turned out.

With neither cup nor measuring spoon in sight, she'd heap a mound of flour on her wooden bread board, poke a hole like a volcano cone in the middle of it, pour in some water and add salt and just a pinch of baking powder, and then start working the gluey ingredients with her hands until she had a sheet of something that, if she were making it today, I'd recognize as pasta. Rolled out flat, sliced into two-inch squares, and simmered in rich chicken broth, those little pillows of dough were love on the tongue, the ultimate comfort food.

Hettie Viola Hillen Morton was really my great-grandmother. It was only after one of her older daughters, Ovie Pearl, turned up "in the family way" that they found out the man who'd been squiring her about was married. So, the baby, my mother, was raised as the last of Grandma's long line of girls.

Once, when my mother and I had driven the twenty miles or so out to the country to see the folks, Grandma asked me if I wanted to help make her specialty. I must have been about six.

"Yes, ma'am," I said. "Want me to get some eggs out of the hen house?"

"We'll see to the eggs in a little while, Sister, but first we need a chicken," she said, handing me a calico bonnet, so I wouldn't get a sunburn out of doors, or heaven forbid, more freckles.

Grandma took me by the hand as we walked out toward the brushy hedge on the far side of the house. She had a big wood fire burning with a tin washtub of water heating

---

**Theresa May** is Editor-in-Chief at the University of Texas Press, where she has worked for nearly thirty years. She has formally studied art history, anthropology, English, and applied piano. In other lives, she is or has been a toymaker, theater costumer, piano teacher, performer, and writer. She is a published poet and a member of the Wordweavers chapter of SCN in Austin, where she lives with her husband, Juan Miranda, and their daughter, Kate.

on it. The yard was a veritable industry of plump hens and busy pullets and one motley, self-important rooster, but I didn't make the connection between those noisy, helter-skelter egg-machines and the scrawny, naked, store-bought carcasses my momma cut up and fried at home.

"Think you can catch one of the hens?" she asked.

"I can try," I answered gamely.

"Never mind. I'll get us one," Grandma said, motioning for me to be quiet, her shadow hovering in front of her like a dark angel and her veiny right hand a lightning strike to the fat Rhode Island White scratching and pecking in the dirt at her feet. That hen didn't even have time for a decent come-to-Jesus squawk before Grandma jerked it up by the neck, whirled it a couple of snappy loop-the-loops in front of her, and after the briefest macabre chase, plopped its headless, twitching body into the boiling bath. The stench of scalding bird feathers made my eyes water. Or, at least that's what I told Grandma, as I watched her fling the hen head, its wide eyes and gaping beak a mirror of my own stunned surprise, into the pigs' slop bucket.

That day was my first hard lesson in the true meaning of food, but it also taught me a lot about the women in my family. Looking back, I wonder what Grandma would have done if that two-timing skunk who'd dipped his carrot in her Ovie-chick's stew had come around the place again. I don't even know his name, but if I did, I guess maybe I'd have to thank him anyway, worthless as he was, for cooking up my sweet momma—and me, the egg in her hen house, her little dumpling.

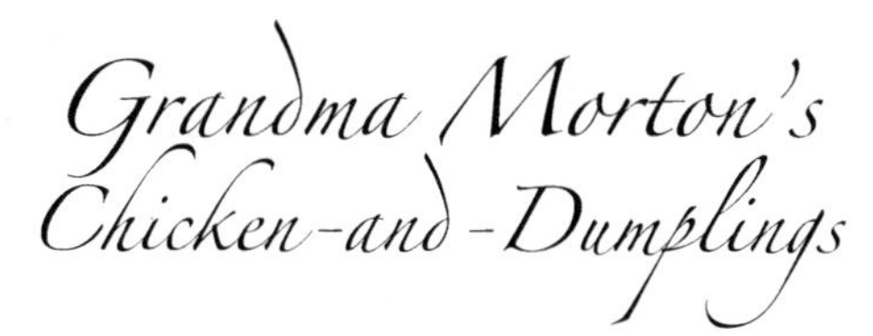


**Ingredients**

| | |
|---|---|
| 1 | chicken, cleaned and cut up |
| 4 | quarts boiling water |
| | Salt and pepper to taste |
| 2 | cups flour |
| 1½ | teaspoons baking powder |
| 1–1½ | cups cold water |

**Preparation**

Clean and cut up a fat hen. In a large pot, simmer the pieces gently in 4 quarts of water until cooked, seasoning to taste. Remove the chicken pieces and set aside to rest. Skim the broth of excess fat or skin bits and reheat to boiling.

On a dough board, make a heaping cone of 2 cups of flour. Poke a hole in the middle; add salt and baking powder. Pour in 1 cup of cold water. Mix by hand, adding more water as needed.

Roll out into smooth flat dough, no more than ⅛ of an inch thick. Cut long strips about 2 inches wide. Then, cut the strips into 2-inch pieces. Drop them into the boiling broth to cook.

Add chicken pieces (skinned and deboned, if you prefer) back to the broth to reheat. If the broth is too thin, stir in a paste made of flour and water to thicken, and adjust seasoning, if needed. Serve hot in bowls.

Serves 5–6.

# *Basil on My Mind*

**Josephine Sherfy**

What's on my mind? The thoughts that come to all gardeners after Valentine's Day! The rake comes out of the garage along with the clippers, shovel, and the tall can to compost leaves and cuttings.

My first after-winter cleanup began a few days ago with that usual sense of outdoor vigor. Every stroke and pull of the rake gave me added energy. As I worked along, I began to think about plant choices for the coming summer garden. I love clay pots with white flowers. In my mind's eye, I can already see a big pot filled with white vinca settled among the roses. My thoughts go on to outdoor plant stores, opening soon with their usual spring display of herbs. I will begin my usual search for a collection of culinary and ornamental basils. I think of shiny big-leaf Greek and Italian with summer tomatoes. The flavors of spicy Thai, chocolate, lemon, and cinnamon basil are a cook's delight. African Blue, bushy and fragrant, blooms until winter's first frost.

I had been in the garden most of the day. I began to feel that chill that comes with March afternoons. I surveyed my large pile of raked leaves, acorns, moss, and twigs. I thought with fatigue, "That's enough for today. Another good day is forecast for tomorrow."

It was then that I saw my wonderful stand of winter-dried fountain grass. I had the usual gardener's doubts. Is it dead? Should I pull it out for compost or leave it for another week with hope for tiny new green shoots? As I contemplated possible survival of the grass with another summer of pink feathery plumes, I saw a clump of winter-dead African Blue basil, leaves long gone. African Blue is my favorite summer cut flower. The blue–green leaves and long-stemmed cones of lavender–blue blossoms project a fragrance that can fill a room. In the fall, bees cover the plant with adoration to harvest the most elegant of all honeys.

I reached out and pulled the unresisting dried basil stalks from the ground. In that brief moment, I was enveloped with the pungent spicy fragrance of fresh basil. Dead? I questioned, how could there be this powerful odor of basil? I placed my gloved hands to my nose. Nothing? There were no leaves. The stems were dry. I held the soil-encrusted roots in my hand. I manipulated the dry roots with my fingers, and there again was that identifiable essence of basil. Those moments were a soul-filling garden experience for me. It was confirmation that a garden with basil has rewards beyond cookbooks and flower arrangements.

---

**Josephine Sherfy** recently returned to her native Austin, after living for fifty-five years in the Washington, DC, area. She enjoys gardening and is now, by trial and error, learning the process of plant survival in Texas summers. She finds that placing a rain umbrella over a favorite day lily plant, during the heat of mid-day, promises more beautiful blooms.

# *Baked Whole Chicken Breast with Basil*

## Ingredients

| | |
|---|---|
| 1 | whole chicken breast, skinless, boneless, and large enough to serve 4 people |
| 2 | cloves garlic, large |
| | Olive oil |
| | Curry powder, mild or medium |
| | Cumin |
| | Black pepper |
| 1 | small onion, chopped |
| ½ | sweet red pepper, chopped |
| ½ | cup Thai basil leaves |
| ¼ | cup chicken broth |

## Preparation

Preheat oven to 325°F.

Line a baking pan with a length of foil large enough to wrap the chicken. Place the washed and dried breast on the bottom of the foil-lined pan.

Prepare a mixture of 2 large cloves of fresh-squeezed garlic and olive oil. Generously brush the mix on the chicken. Dust well with curry powder (not "hot") and cumin. Sprinkle with ground black pepper.

Top the chicken with a small chopped onion, the chopped sweet red pepper, and ½ cup of fresh washed Thai basil leaves. Add ¼ cup of chicken broth around the base of the chicken breast.

Enclose chicken breast, seasonings, and broth in the foil, making a package around the chicken. Place in preheated oven.

Bake approximately 1 hour at 325°F. If you wish to check earlier for doneness, peek and pierce chicken with a knife. The juices should run clear. If the chicken needs to cook longer, reseal the package and continue baking.

Serve slices of chicken with juices on a bed of cooked rice and fresh, washed arugula.

Serves 4.

## Tips and Notes

These are a few of my favorite flavors and uses for culinary basil:

Italian and Greek Basil—These are most often used in Mediterranean foods from Italy, France, Spain, North Africa, Greece, and Turkey.

Cinnamon Basil—This flavor is good chopped fine and sprinkled into fresh fruits. You may also top the fruit and basil with vanilla yogurt.

Chocolate Basil—Chocolate basil is wonderful chopped fine and sprinkled into fresh fruits. This is also good topped with vanilla yogurt.

Lemon Basil—Lemon basil is great served with fresh fish, vegetables, and pastas or salads.

Thai Basil—Thai basil is spicy, associated with foods of Southeast Asia, India, and Indonesia.

African Blue—African Blue basil is a beautiful cut flower to arrange alone or mix with summer flowers.

# Big Sis Carolyn's Creative Kitchen

**Bonnie Watkins**

She saved my life, more than once. The first time, she saved me literally. In our country frame house, central heat or air was unknown. We relied on space heaters to dull the damp cold of January. Daddy lit them at four a.m. when he got up to go to the dairy barn for morning milking. When we got up at six to get ready for our one-hour rural bus ride, the chill had somewhat left the house, but it would never be totally warm because the high ceilings craved more and more heat. In fact, anyone who ever cozied up to a space heater knows its mechanics: the side of you facing the heater is roasting and the other side, just inches away, is freezing. Still we tried to get warm by backing closer to the heater. That January morning of 1958, I nestled closer and closer until—whoosh—the back of my chenille robe burst into flames. Remember, this happened before the days when all children knew the drill of "Stop, drop, and roll!" Carolyn, my older sister, instinctively knew what to do. She tackled me to the ground and rolled me around on the linoleum floor until the flames died.

She saved me countless other times, emotionally. On picture day at school when my ponytail came down, I ran to her with the brush, and she repaired it. She talked me through the Cuban Missile Crisis, my fear of atomic bombs, and the sorrow of dead puppies. Before I went to school, she provided a lifeline to the learning that I already loved. Born early to my current teacher profession, most days found me teaching whatever willing or captive student I could find. Sometimes I dressed up the dogs and sat them on the picnic bench to hear the 3Rs. Other times my dolls listened as I read long stories. When Carolyn arrived home, she unloaded her notebook with paper, pens, rulers, colored pencils, and all the other fascinating tools of the trade. In addition, we traded roles and I became her most willing pupil. Before I reached first grade (no kindergarten then in country schools), I could read and multiply and divide, as well as add and subtract. She nourished my curious mind years before Mama and Daddy made the sacrifices to send me to college to become a teacher.

Carolyn's calling was art. She drove the pick-up truck down country roads to visit Mrs. Lane, a "neighbor" five miles away, who first taught her art. I remember Carolyn's oil paintings set up against Mrs. Lane's hedges to dry.

Carolyn brought that same artistry to cooking. Her meals were always colorful and beautiful, as well as delicious. During the summer months, my boys, Brian and Phillip, and I used to visit her in Dallas. They loved her pool and I loved the pampering I got from our cooking together, where she did most of the work and I sat on a kitchen stool and talked to her!

Artists thrive on creativity, and so does Carolyn's cooking. She's not afraid to experiment and most of her recipes that I like best were experiments where she just thought, "I bet that this and that would taste good together." Here are two I learned from her.

---

**Bonnie Watkins** has been a teacher all of her life, teaching ages two to ninety-two. Currently, she teaches American Literature, Communication Applications, and Creative Writing at Hyde Park Baptist High School in Austin, Texas. For several years, she wrote a monthly column, "Making Money at Home," for *Welcome Home* magazine. She has published parenting and teaching articles, as well as poems and devotionals. Bonnie belongs to the Wordweavers Story Circle Network writing circle in Austin.

# Chicken and Leeks

### Ingredients

- 6 pieces chicken, breasts or thighs or a mixture of both
- 2 leeks, washed and sliced
- 2 carrots, washed and chopped
- 1 10-ounce can condensed tomato soup
- ½ soup can water

### Preparation

Brown the cut-up chicken pieces in olive oil in a skillet.

Chop 2 leeks, slicing both the white and green parts, to the end of the stem. Put the leeks in a colander and wash well, because dirt lodges between the leaves. Also, chop 2 carrots and wash. Scatter the chopped leeks and carrots around the chicken in the skillet, and add one can of condensed tomato soup and the ½ can of water.

Cover. Simmer about 30 minutes, until the leeks and carrots are tender and the chicken is cooked.

Serves 6.

### Tips and Notes

You may use skinless and/or boneless chicken for this recipe to reduce the fat content.

Serve the chicken on a bed of rice or noodles, if desired.

# Avocado Salad

### Ingredients

- 1 bunch green-leaf or red-tipped lettuce, washed, dried, and torn into pieces
- 2 avocados, peeled and sliced
- 4 hard-boiled eggs, chopped
- ½ cup mayonnaise
- 2 tablespoons mustard
- ¼ teaspoon salt
- ¼ teaspoon pepper
- ¼ cup (or enough to achieve desired consistency) dill pickle juice, drained from pickles

### Preparation

Make a bed of green-leaf or red-tipped lettuce, and lay the avocado slides on top.

Next, make the dressing (here's the creative and best part). Chop hard-boiled eggs, add mayonnaise, mustard, and salt and pepper to taste (essentially, make egg salad). Thin this mixture with dill pickle juice to your desired consistency of salad dressing; some like it thicker, others prefer more liquid. Pour over the lettuce and avocados. Serve cold.

Serves 6.

# *Hockey Pucks*

**Jane Cadieux**

A breaded patty made from minced chicken, eggs, and garlic, fried to a crispy golden brown is one of the most treasured foods in my extended family. Phonetically spelled, these patties are known in our family as *fusheers*, but I have no idea where that word came from or what it means. Even after searching in cookbooks of both Hungarian and Jewish cuisines, I could not find anything that remotely resembles that word.

The recipe emigrated from Hungary before the First World War with my grandfather, his two brothers, and his sister Helen. Auntie Helen first introduced these tasty little patties, light as air and fried to perfection, to her immediate family. As her brothers began to take wives from outside the tightly-knit Hungarian circle in their new city, the *fusheer* evolved. When my grandfather married Sadie, born from freshly transplanted Byelorussian émigrés, the *fusheer* morphed into a whole different food group—something we came to know as…hockey pucks.

Grandma was not the most delicate of cooks and certainly didn't have the culinary finesse that Auntie Helen had. Grandma's *fusheers* were always a little flatter, a little harder, and a little more burnt than Auntie Helen's. They were also very garlicky and made with a cornflake crumb crust, rather than a breadcrumb crust, which I can only assume was Grandma's own variation on the theme, as she was happy to use ingredients from the New World. I am also not sure who came up with "hockey pucks," but this left-handed term of endearment wasn't much of a stretch, and so the name stuck.

Sadie was plagued with arthritis, which worked and twisted her fingers into painful knots. On Sabbath, she painted her nails peach, which only accentuated her deformity. Perhaps it was the arthritis that resulted in the *fusheer* turned hockey puck, or it could have been because she employed Grandpa to do most of the mixing and shaping.

Grandma, a five-foot, rounded figure with large glasses, would still be wearing her floral apron when she came through the swinging door from the kitchen with the large platter of these little marvels, setting them ceremoniously on the table that had been dressed with her best Sabbath linens, china, and cutlery. We grandchildren would yell in unison, "Yea! Hockey pucks!" as if we had just received manna that had fallen from heaven and crashed through the roof. She laughed with us and was actually proud of this seemingly insulting moniker leveled at her cooking. We would tuck in, even before the rest of the platters arrived. There would be a lot of food—chicken soup with boiled chicken, vegetables, and matzo balls (we called her matzo balls, sinkers), a large brisket of beef, sides of potato knishes, carrot tsimmes, (a sweet carrot dish), and noodle pudding. We were never sure if the hockey pucks were a main course, side dish, or appetizer. Sometimes they came after the soup but before the main course and sometimes in tandem with the vegetables. Nevertheless, the tray had to be replenished several times, right up until dessert.

When I was older and traveling, Grandma would

---

**Jane Cadieux** started out in the business world as a fashion designer/merchandiser. After one marriage, two children, three international moves, and living life for the past thirteen years overseas, she evolved into a wife, mother, teacher, volunteer, photographer, artist, writer... observer.

sometimes give me a care package of cold hockey puck sandwiches to take on the plane—something akin to a "fast-food chicken burger" except that these were wedged between challah or *kimmel* bread, smeared with strong mustard, and wreaking of garlic. I was forced to consume them quickly at the airport, so strong was the smell of garlic permeating from the tightly foil-wrapped contents, further protected in a Ziploc bag claiming to lock in freshness. People near me stared and grimaced as if I possessed a dangerous weapon.

The *fusheer* will always be clouded in mystery, both in name and meal placement. Even the recipe varies. Quantities were not important. It was something you felt. They might have been part of the cuisine of my grandfather's village or just a family word. Certainly, the breaded chicken patty is common enough. And though the origin of the *fusheer* continues to elude our knowledge, the hockey puck doesn't. It conjures up a very specific image, not just of a black rubber disc slapped around an ice rink, not even of the garlicky cornflake-crusted chicken patty, but of the little round lady with large glasses, floral apron, and gnarled peach-nailed fingers wrapped around the handles of an oversized platter. Maybe our reference to hockey pucks was a bit harsh, but Grandma's ear-to-ear grin when she heard it as she came through the swinging door convinced us that she didn't mind at all.

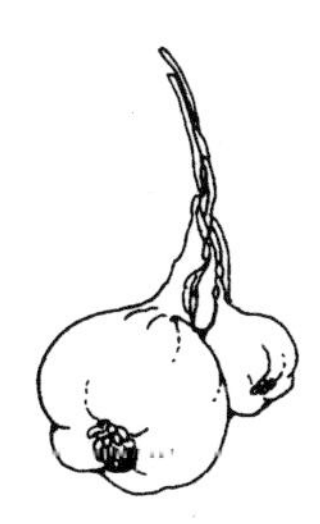

### Recipe Tips and Notes

The quantity of challah is an estimate only. You can use white bread or crushed soda crackers if challah is unavailable.

# Fusheers or Hockey Pucks

## (Chicken Patties)

### Ingredients

- 3 pounds boneless, skinless, chicken breast, raw and minced
- 2 large eggs
- 5–6 slices challah (egg bread), crusts removed, slightly dampened, and broken
- 1 large clove minced garlic (or to taste)
- Salt and pepper to taste
- 1 large onion, chopped finely
- Oil for frying
- Breadcrumbs or cornflake crumbs

### Preparation

Preheat oven to 375°F.

To the minced chicken, add the eggs, challah, garlic, and salt and pepper. Mix these ingredients together by hand or in a food processor. Set aside this mixture while you brown the chopped onion in a little oil. Add the onion to the batter and mix well. The batter will be sticky. Take generous spoonfuls of the mixture and shape into balls. Dip them into the crumbs. Then, press lightly into hockey pucks. Turn to coat both sides with crumbs.

Brown the patties in hot oil for 2–3 minutes until golden brown. Turn them over and brown the other side. The patties will not be cooked through at this stage. Put the pucks on a cookie sheet and bake in the oven at 375°F. for 45 minutes or until done. The patties will continue to brown in the oven.

Yields about 3-dozen small pucks.

# K38 Kook-King

**Shawn Alladio**

*Shawn Alladio teaches swiftwater rescue skills to firefighters and other emergency personnel through her company, K38 Water Safety. Now, Shawn has added a new workshop to the K38 Water Safety offerings with a back-to-basics cooking class. LOL**

This class teaches emergency rescue personnel to "camp on site–eat on site" when called to remote rescue locations. So let's set the scene for those readers who shiver at the thought of camping, never mind a swim in an icy river.

The perfect setting is Pine Flat Dam on the King's River in California. King's River is cold and enticing, yet dangerous. In early spring, the snow melt pushes the water hard and fast, so a shlug-shlug sound accompanies the crackling of the campfire.

To visualize this class, imagine a blonde, athletic woman, five-foot six, leading a group of twenty-four men, heroic lifesaving types, some of whom are out of shape, obviously eating too much, and not doing enough to keep their physical charms in proportion. Then, throw in a few gems who flex their biceps because they still can (those are few and far between).

Ideally, this class will take place on an extremely cold day. The colder it is, the more they complain. I've found the only two ways to make an unhappy man happy: first, keep their bellies full; second, keep their balls empty. I refrain from the latter. If I didn't, my cooking class would have to have PayPal fees attached.

Next, I work them harder than some of them have worked in years. Keep in mind, the location removes all wives, girlfriends, titty bars, and refrigerators within a fifty-mile radius. This creates a hunger that'll induce a man to eat anything, even a petrified Cliff Bar, especially when he hasn't come prepared because he thought this class would be all fluff. After all, a *woman* teaches it.

I always warn the men to bring food, but our group inspection of gear reveals ice chests firmly topped off with beer—and no food. Typical male behavior! Lucky for them, their female instructor (yours truly) thinks ahead and has food and a gigantic $39 roll of Costco foil ready to rumble.

Pine Flat Dam is far enough from any civilized restaurant to force the men to campfire cooking. It is considered cheating to have the Fresno Fire Department bring out their huge barbecues built on portable trailers. Luxury is not an option. Everyone must suffer and hunger for this meal to truly be the best they ever had.

Now, for the real action; here's how to create the necessary hunger. First, send the men to gather plenty of wood and rocks; we are living off the land for this class.

*Continues on page 74*

---

**Shawn Alladio**, age forty-six and a Californian, is the proud mother of two daughters, Shaniah, age three, and Kyla, age twenty-five. She enjoys life from the offbeat perspective of a deep and sometimes awkward soul. Shawn currently navigates the school of life through various global pursuits, including working in water rescue with her company, K38 Water Safety. She also shares life with her unknowing muse Ray Wolfgramm. Shawn's personal motto is, "The life you save may be your own."

* LOL means "laughing out loud."

# *Shawn's K38 Campfire Chicken*

### Ingredients

| | |
|---|---|
| | Heavy-duty aluminum foil (1 giant roll or 2 regular rolls) |
| 20 | medium red potatoes, washed, 2 per serving |
| 10 | cloves garlic, peeled and sliced |
| 3 | sweet yellow onions, large, sliced |
| 4 | pounds carrots, 3-inch pieces, cleaned |
| 10 | big pieces skinless chicken, leg quarters work best |
| 20 | ounces olive oil, ¼ cup per serving |
| 20 | ounces barbecue sauce, ¼ cup per serving |
| 2 | teaspoons rosemary |
| 2 | teaspoons poultry seasoning |
| 2 | teaspoons thyme or basil |
| 1 | teaspoon salt |
| 1 | teaspoon pepper |
| 1–2 | bunches parsley, washed and torn into small pieces |
| 3⅓ | cups water, ⅓ cup per serving |

### Preparation

Start a campfire, and surround it with large rocks. Let it burn to create hot coals and hot rocks for cooking while you prepare the dinner packets.

Make 10 big flat pieces of foil (each 3 times the width of the food in each direction, to allow for steam) using at least 2 large sheets of foil each. Fold the foil together securely at the edges, with the shiny side facing out. Spray the inside with nonstick spray. Divide the potatoes and veggies equally among the packets. Then, rinse the chicken pieces and place on top of the veggies.

Now, pull the foil up into a bowl shape. Smother everything with olive oil and barbecue sauce.

Next, blend the spices, salt and pepper, and parsley together. Then, divide evenly between the packets and sprinkle the seasoning mix over the meat and vegetables. Pour the water around the edges. Don't wash the sauce and spices off the food. Seal each packet by folding the top of the foil firmly, to seal tight. Plop it above hot coals—**not** over flames.

Support the packets with large rocks or a grate, but **don't** set the bags directly on the coals. You can make a teepee of foil to put over the top of the entire fire pit to capture and radiate the heat. This speeds up the cooking, which can take several hours. It depends on the heat of the fire and how many people you're feeding.

After about an hour, open a packet carefully to check (caution: steam is very hot). When chicken juices run clear, dinner is done.

Serves 10.

### Tips and Notes

You may also cook this dish on your home barbecue. Just set the packets on the grill and use low heat. Arrange the packets so the heat will be indirect or turn the fire down low enough that it does not touch the foil.

You may create one packet for two or more people for convenience. Just be careful that the packets are not too heavy to handle safely. We don't recommend making 1 giant packet to feed a large number of people!

*Continued from page 72*

Surprisingly, it's not a problem finding a match to start a fire—most firemen are smokers. Isn't that weird?

Next, build a very hot fire and place a lot of large rocks tight around the perimeter. Let the rocks get good and hot; they have to provide heat to cook the food for hours, while I am at the river's edge yelling to the men, *"Stand up, Operator, stand up! You cannot balance that boat if you are sitting down!"* This exercise really helps build their appetites.

After the men spend hours in a near-freezing river, where they've been immersed in icy water, pelted with cold wind, and nearly frozen their hands off, they become a scraggly group that looks like they just survived Armageddon. They'll return to camp with rosy cheeks and haggard faces, searching for food. (The TV show, *Survivor*, is all fluff and entertainment; waterside camp training is the real test of a man's conditioning!)

During our lunch break, I return to camp to prepare a meal that will cook while we work in the afternoon, after teasing the men with promises of a lovely barbecue for the evening meal. This also teases their appetites, which forces them to dig into their knapsacks to scrounge up the fruit they don't want to eat.

For our campfire meal, I make a huge flat piece of foil from multiple sheets of aluminum foil, folded securely together at the edges. (This oversize piece will eventually look like an old stove-popped popcorn foil ball.) Then, I double check to make sure no seams will come open; all the juices have to be caught up inside, to create a swirl of blended flavors.

Next, I add a bunch of veggies, top them with meat, toss seasonings on top, and seal the foil packet. I plop it into the fire pit, just above the hot coals. Then, I make a teepee of foil to put over the top. Cooking this gigantic packet can take hours; it depends on how many people you're feeding. With twenty-four men to feed, this project is huge—and ridiculous looking.

When you smell it, it's done!

I finish out the meal with cans of Bush's baked beans (no, I'm not going to make beans; there's a reason I tell everyone to bring a can opener), a box of minute rice, and a can of Progresso peeled tomatoes to add to the rice. It doesn't matter whether the rice turns out lumpy, sticky, dry, cracked, or has dirt in it. They won't notice. I also make it with a foil bag, like the chicken. I'll be damned if I'm going to wash dishes in a campsite.

Hand out the food. Then sit back and watch the men suck on them chicken bones. When they are relaxed and have their bellies full, it's time for night operations training! We now train until two a.m., into the wee hours of their normal sleeping routine. They don't call me Hell-Woman for nuttin'!

---

**Regina Moser,** the author of "Turkey Leftovers," wears many hats. She is professionally known as a Job Search Coach, Yoga Instructor, and Spiritual Director. Regina feels her personal mission is to encourage growth in herself and others, and she is forever encouraging people to write and tell their stories. She loves to read and cook, and she's fascinated by small world stories of connection. Known as the "Email Queen," she shares her joy in writing with family and friends.

# *Turkey Leftovers*

**Regina Moser**

As Mike and I were shopping the turkey deals at the local grocery store, we were faced with the dilemma of buying a mammoth sized bird for our small Thanksgiving celebration. I began to protest, thinking, what am I going to do with all the leftovers? I love turkey leftovers, but everything in moderation. It's just the two of us after the kids go back to school. Mike whispered two words in my ear—"Tortilla soup." A smile came to my face, "Ahhh, yes, tortilla soup."

It brings back the memory and joy of creating homemade turkey broth, picking the turkey meat from the bones, finding the wish bone, breathing the aroma as the house fills with the smell of simmering broth, playing with the recipe by substituting the homemade broth for the cans of broth, using fresh jalapeno in the soup, topping the soup bowls with coarsely chopped cilantro and a squeeze of fresh lime, enjoying this recipe, which has been played with and developed to contain subtle layers of flavor yet is open to more play—*á la* Rachael Ray.

When we lived in El Paso, we were blessed with many friends. Some of our dearest friends shared with us the joy of tortilla soup. Diane and Patti were both great cooks, and I have many fond memories of sharing many bowls of tortilla soup with them. Patti was a dear woman and wrote the recipe down for me. Here it is to share with you.

The legend of the tortilla soup recipe grows when I send it out to friends and family as a gift email after Thanksgiving. Many friends have tried and played with this recipe and say "yum" to this awesome soup and continue to play—cause some like it hot.

# *Tortilla Soup*

**Ingredients**

| | |
|---|---|
| 1 | medium onion, chopped |
| 1 | jalapeno, chopped |
| 2 | cloves garlic, minced |
| 2 | tablespoons cooking oil |
| 2 | pounds cooked turkey, shredded |
| 1 | 14-ounce can tomatoes |
| 1 | 5-ounce can Rotel tomatoes and green chilies |
| 1¼ | cups beef broth |
| 1¼ | cups chicken broth |
| 1 | 10-ounce can tomato soup |
| 1½ | soup cans water |
| 1 | 14-ounce can tomato sauce |
| 1 | teaspoon ground cumin |
| 1 | teaspoon chili powder |
| ½ | teaspoon lemon–pepper seasoning |
| 2 | teaspoons Worcestershire sauce |
| 1 | teaspoon Tabasco sauce |

**Preparation**

Sauté the first 5 ingredients in a large kettle. Add the remaining ingredients and simmer for 1 hour. Pour into bowls and top with tortilla chips, shredded cheese, avocado, green onions, and sour cream, if desired.

Serves 6–8.

**Tips and Notes**

The fresh jalapeno can be substituted with a small can of diced jalapenos.

# The Longest Hour

**Beth van Duzer**

"That's it!" I say exasperated. "There will be no TV for the rest of the evening."

"Why, Mommy?" asks my whiny three year old.

"Because you hit me in the head with your sister's blanket and it hurt my eye, that's why. I expect you to play nicely while I am making dinner, no crying, no complaining."

Off I go to make Fish Pie for dinner. Everything seems to be running smoothly for the first five minutes until I hear off in the distance: "Get off of me. Get off of me. *Get off of me!*"

"Lucy? Is that you?" I ask, as I am measuring frozen vegetables.

As if by magic, my daughter appears next to me stating, "Mommy, I have poop on my butt."

I look at her. She has her underwear on. I sigh deeply. "Okay, let's go to the bathroom." As I clean up my daughter, I proceed to lecture her: "Lucy, honey, next time just ask Mommy for help. Now, go upstairs and get new underwear and come right back."

"Okay, Mommy," my daughter says happily.

Note to self: don't forget that her soiled underwear is in the sink. Now, it's back to washing my hands and making dinner. Recipe says to strain the milk and pour it into the flour and butter mixture. Let me do that.

"Lucy, where are you? What is making that beeping noise? Did you touch the computer? Get over here. Ugh!" I just spilled the milk. I would debate about crying over it, but the computer is beeping incessantly and my daughter is not responding. "Lucy!"

"Uhm…I touched a switch," my daughter says sheepishly.

"Get over here. You need to find a book to read by yourself *now*."

Let me turn everything on the stove to low and see if I can get this beeping to stop. Unplugging the computer and plugging it in again doesn't work. Hmm, let me call my husband.

"Hi, honey, do you have a minute? Well, Lucy touched a switch and now your computer is beeping relentlessly. Yes, I did unplug it. Why would I need to turn a switch off if I unplugged it? Okay, I'll try it and…Lucy, what are you doing to your sister? Leave her alone! Sorry, wait, no. It is still beeping. Look, I'm just going to unplug it. I have to go."

I rushed back to the sink to wash my hands. What was I doing? Oh, the milk. I'll clean it up once the stove is off. My luck I'll just wind up in the emergency room if I try to clean it now. The recipe calls for homemade mashed potatoes. No time—instant will do. It needs chives? Who really eats chives anyway? Oops, there's a crying one year old under my feet.

"Lola, honey, Mommy can't give you dinner until it's finished cooking. Do you want something to drink? How

---

**Beth van Duzer** is a stay-at-home mom in Georgetown, Massachusetts. In her free time, she reads, writes, and is copresident of her local mothers' club, *The Mother Connection*. She submits stories of her family's mishaps to this club's newsletter as well as *Motherwords*, a regional magazine. Her oldest daughter frequently tells her, and anyone who will listen, how much she dislikes fish pie.

# Fish Pie

### Ingredients

- 3–4 cups mashed potatoes
- 1 pound fresh cod, skinless
- 3¾ cups milk
- 1 bay leaf
- 1 parsley sprig
- 4 tablespoons butter
- 1 onion, finely chopped
- 3 tablespoons flour
- 1 teaspoon dry mustard
- 1 cup green peas
- 1 cup corn kernels
- 1 tablespoon snipped fresh chives
- 4 tablespoons grated Cheddar cheese
- Salt and pepper to taste

### Preparation

Preheat the oven to 350°F.

Prepare the mashed potatoes and set aside.

Place the fish in a shallow pan with the milk, bay leaf, and parsley. Bring to a boil. Cover and cook for 5 minutes or until the fish flakes easily. Remove the fish, and strain and reserve the milk. Flake the fish with a fork and set aside.

Melt the butter in a medium pan, add the onion, and sauté until softened. Stir in the flour to make a paste, and cook for 1 minute. Gradually add the strained milk, stirring until the sauce thickens.

Mix in the mustard, peas, corn, chives, and 2 tablespoons of Cheddar cheese. Cook for 4 minutes. Season to taste and add the fish.

Put the mixture in an 11x7-inch ovenproof dish. Spread the mashed potatoes over the fish, making peaks with a fork. Sprinkle with the remaining cheese. Bake for 25 minutes at 350°F. Serves 6.

### Tips and Notes

For homemade mashed potatoes, boil potatoes until tender. Mash and add milk, butter, water, salt, and pepper, as desired.

You may use instant mashed potatoes instead of cooking and mashing fresh potatoes. Follow the directions on the package.

This dish is suitable for freezing.

For an interesting variation, add cooked shrimp to the fish.

You can also make miniature portions in ramekin dishes.

---

about some water? Oh, sweetie, please stop crying. Here, have a cracker."

Yup, instant potatoes with butter sound fine to me. I think I can put this in the oven. Why is it so quiet?

"Lucy, where is your sister?"

"Uhm…in the closet."

I shake my head, sigh deeply again, rescue the one year old, and tell my older daughter, "Give Mommy five more minutes, and then I am yours. Here, let's use the stopwatch. You can see how fast Mommy cleans up." At this point, I'll do anything to get her away from her sister. Let's see: take underwear upstairs and throw into washing machine, clean up spilled milk.... What's that new beeping noise?

"Mommy, time's up."

Looks like pots and pans will have to wait.

# A Family Tradition

**Penny Appleby**

"Tradition" is a song in *Fiddler on the Roof* that speaks to the main theme of the story—how everyone in the family is impacted by cultural as well as family traditions. Every family has traditions, recurring events usually associated with holidays, that bind them together and are the threads that knit the family together through the years.

I would guess that most family traditions center on food in some way. There is the Thanksgiving menu that is pretty much the same from year to year. There is the cake that is baked for special occasions, the Saturday morning special breakfast of pancakes, and the special birthday meal. Sometimes, the special food is associated with a particular person—my father's favorite cake. But I suspect that most of the time, it's hard to remember when the tradition started. Years will pass and all of a sudden, you realize that you always have a certain food for a specific occasion—a tradition—and you begin to honor it and to maintain it.

We have several traditional foods in our family, but there is one that is most special to me. I can't really tell you when it began, but I can say that for more than twenty years, we've enjoyed this particular treat every Christmas. The recipe is the result of a visit to an excellent (five stars at that time) restaurant in New Orleans called Mosca's. (I haven't been there in many years, but it is still there.)

At the time we went to Mosca's, my brother and his family lived in Slidell, Louisiana, just across Lake Pontchartrain from New Orleans. Our family-style Italian Creole meal consisted of a cracked crab salad and chicken. I don't remember having the oysters there. It was probably the next Christmas, when we were at my brother's (another tradition after he married and had kids), that my sister-in-law, Eve, prepared this dish for the first time. I'm not sure how she came to have the recipe. I have seen it in a cookbook that I have from Kentucky, though it's not quite the same as our dish. I'm not even sure if ours is just like what is served in the restaurant; no matter, it's our traditional dish.

When my brother and I were growing up, we were encouraged to try all foods. Our parents' philosophy was that if you didn't taste it you wouldn't know whether you liked it or not. Growing up in Columbus, Georgia, provided access to and knowledge of some good basic food—this was before Julia Child taught America about French cooking. In addition to the standard staples of pork, beef, chicken, peas, turnip greens, sweet potatoes, and grits, I learned to like souse meat, brains, and cracklings; you can see that to me oysters are not an unusual or undesirable food. On the contrary, they are one of my favorites of all the foods of the sea, and ice cold and raw is my favorite way to eat them. This love of all kinds of food is pretty much true of the entire family—it was very easy for

---

**Penny Appleby** is retired and lives in Austin, Texas (though she grew up in Georgia). She loves to eat and to cook and has an extensive cookbook collection. In addition to serving as the Secretary-Treasurer of Story Circle Network, Penny is a docent at the Austin Museum of Art, sings in the choir at the First United Methodist Church, is a member of local American History Club, a reading mentor at a local grammar school, and plays bridge every other week.

Oysters Mosca to become a family tradition.

Even though some may not eat the bivalves raw, they may partake of them after they have been cooked. For those in this category, Mosca is a wonderful way to serve oysters—the accompanying flavors of olive oil, butter, garlic, and cheese will tempt most everyone.

We always serve this dish mid-afternoon on Christmas Day as an appetizer for our Christmas dinner. In the early years, it was usually prepared by Eve, but eventually it became my treat to buy the ingredients and make the dish as my contribution to our Christmas eating. Also, I feel that I owe Eve for having provided the recipe in the first place. A particularly good accompaniment to the dish is a cold glass of champagne, with which to toast everyone a Merry Christmas. Well, almost everyone enjoys the Mosca; did I forget to mention that Eve doesn't eat oysters!

# Oysters Mosca

### Ingredients

| | |
|---|---|
| | Italian breadcrumbs |
| 2 | pints oysters |
| 3 | cloves or more garlic, minced |
| | Parmesan cheese, grated |
| | Romano cheese, grated |
| ½ | stick butter (approx.) |
| 2 | tablespoons olive oil |

### Preparation

Preheat the oven to 350°F.

Sprinkle enough breadcrumbs to cover the bottom of a 13x9x2-inch greased dish. Layer the oysters on top of the breadcrumbs. Sprinkle the garlic on top of the oysters. Sprinkle enough of both cheeses to cover the top. Sprinkle again with breadcrumbs.

Melt the butter, add the olive oil, and pour the mixture over the breadcrumbs. Use more butter and olive oil, if necessary. Bake at 350°F. for approximately 30–40 minutes, until the top is browned.

Serves 6–8, as an appetizer.

### Tips and Notes

As with our stories, which happen mostly in the telling, this recipe happens in the preparation. There is room for interpretation and invention.

# *It's Not Your Everyday Soul Food*

**Teddy Broeker**

Food is sustenance for the body and also nourishment for the soul. In this sense, under the right conditions, any food can be soul food, particularly when it is shared with someone special. I remember a lonely time in my life, when we had moved to the country. My husband traveled a lot, at least half of the month, so I was alone in the middle of nowhere. Actually, I felt quite lost.

I met Tina at church. I noticed that we both sat alone, so I asked if I could join her. This led to our friendship. At ninety, Tina lived alone, taking care of her own home—incredible! I was forty years younger and struggling with my living arrangements because of being uprooted—transplanted in alien soil; there was Tina managing beautifully. What an example she was!

I soon learned that Tina had lost her driver, a neighbor she had relied on to take her shopping and to doctors appointments. With time on my hands, I was happy to help her. Tina was very grateful and I was soon able to understand her thinking when we would market on Tuesday and she would invite me to "dinner" (at noon) on Wednesday. Sharing her meals was Tina's way of thanking me. For me, it was one meal in a lonely week when I had companionship. More than my needing a friend, I did not want Tina to feel that she owed me anything. Since I had refused money for helping her, I knew she wanted to be on level ground with me, and so we dined at her small kitchen table.

Tina and I may have seemed an odd pair, but the arrangement worked for both of us. The food was simple fare because Tina was receiving commodities due to her financial circumstances. There was very little fresh food because of the cost of freshness. Isn't that a crying shame? Dinner was delicious nonetheless, and we became good friends.

At Christmastime, Tina asked me to try some of her famous *lutefisk*. I had heard much about *lutefisk*, because she had gone to considerable effort to obtain the ingredients and had been working on preparations for days. When she explained that it was uncooked fish, I was ready to run.

"It's okay," she said. "It is cured."

I could not tell her that I did not want to try the fish she was so proud of, so try it I did. A taste was all I had, as I learned about Tina's family history and that dried fish was a staple in Sweden. *Lutefisk* was her family's traditional Christmas Eve dinner, and every year she would reconstitute the fish in her kitchen sink.

This sharing experience and the good times we had still warm my heart. At the time, I remember thinking that if I befriended Tina, someone faraway would be kind to my mother—rather like in the saying "what goes around, comes around." I suppose this is because of the associations I have with friendship, food, and Mother.

*Continues on page 82*

---

**Teddy Broeker** is married and has two grown children and four grandchildren. The two oldest grandchildren graduate from high school this May. Teddy went back to school late in life to study psychology and counseling psychology; hence, her interest in relationships. One could say she is a student of human behavior. She loves to witness caring social interactions and of course, loves to be part of them. Teddy says, "This trumps today's consumerism mentality."

# Mediterranean Style Salt Cod

### Ingredients

- 1 pound salt cod
- ¾ pound small potatoes, washed
- 2 tablespoons olive oil
- 1–2 cloves garlic
- 1 green bell pepper
- 1 red bell pepper
- 1 medium onion
- Parsley, chopped
- Olives, green or black, pitted
- Olive oil to taste

### Preparation

**Presoak the salt cod.** A day ahead, place the salt cod in a half-gallon, airtight, plastic container or a large pot and cover with cold water. Store the cod in the refrigerator for 24 hours, changing the water twice to remove the excess salt.

To prepare the dish, drain the pre-soaked cod and place it in a large pot. Cover it again with fresh water. Bring the cod to a boil and simmer for 5 minutes. Using a slotted spoon, remove the cod to a plate. Using a fork, flake the cod into 1–2-inch pieces and set aside.

In the water used to boil the cod, boil the potatoes in their skins. When cooked, set them aside to cool slightly. Cut the potatoes into approximately ¾-inch cubes or pieces.

Slice the garlic cloves thinly, and chop the onion and bell peppers into 1-inch squares. Heat the olive oil over medium heat in a large skillet. Add the garlic, onion, and bell peppers. Sauté until the vegetables have softened slightly.

Add the potatoes and cod to the vegetable mixture and combine everything over a gentle heat until all ingredients are heated through. Adjust the seasoning. Pour into a heated serving dish. Garnish with fresh parsley, pitted olives, and a dash more of olive oil to taste.

Serves 3–4

### Tips and Notes

Look for salt cod in Hispanic grocery stores and some ethnic delicatessens.

Even after soaking the cod, the fish may remain quite salty.

Use extra virgin olive oil for an authentic flavor.

You can also garnish this dish with slices of hard-cooked eggs.

*Continued from page 80*

Food was merely one of the props in our friendship, but food was how Mother loved us.

I don't expect to find a *lutefisk* recipe in any cookbook, but to me it is symbolic of a friendship that I hope was mutually beneficial. It surely fed me. Many years have passed since that time, and I hold memories in my heart of what a good friend Tina was. She taught me a lot, and I believe I can be a better friend today for having known her.

Tina was not a learned friend, but she had a social intelligence that allowed her to respect, care for, and have a warm regard for others. Sometimes we choose our friends because of similarities, our outward appearances. Tina and I were very different on the outside, if worldly evaluations are the consideration. Without such considerations, we were two people who needed each other. As such, we were quite alike, and each was motivated to help the other.

Much like what food does for the body—not due to its appearance but because it sustains us—Tina was like medicine, just what the doctor ordered. She was food for the soul of this lonely person.

There are still a few fish merchants in Minnesota who sell the Norwegian dried cod for homemade *lutefisk*, which is made by reconstituting the dried cod in a lye bath over several weeks. Dried cod and recipes for *lutefisk* can be found on the Internet, for those brave enough to try it.

The Scandinavians also preserved cod using salt, and salt cod became very popular in southern Europe in the days before refrigerators. Many Mediterranean countries—Italy, Portugal, Spain, France—have tasty salt cod dishes. The salt cod in these recipes is much less labor intensive to prepare, is more readily available, and is recommended. So are shared memories and good soul food.

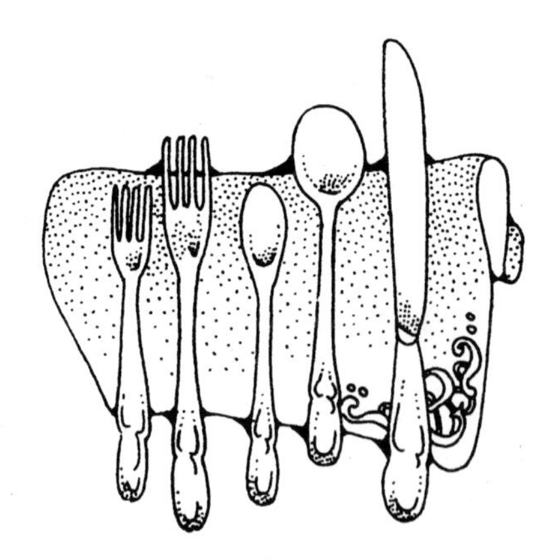

# Meat Dishes

# *Making Gravy*

**Joyce Murray Boatright**

I learned to cook when I was nine. My first menu consisted of chicken-fried steak, cream gravy, mashed potatoes, corn, and green beans.

Momma was my sorcerer. She grew up on a West Texas farm where she learned to snap beans and husk corn and knead bread and twist off the heads of live chickens. I yearned to lay that kind of claim in the kitchen, and I decided the chicken-fried beige plate special was the best place to start. Momma stood nearby to guide my neophyte efforts. Following Momma's directions, I cut up the potatoes and placed them in a pan of blistering water.

Next, I got out the butcher-tenderized minute steaks—called minute steaks I'm sure because they took only minutes to fry up—and dipped them in a bowl of beaten eggs, dredged and dusted them in salt-and-peppered white flour, then dipped and dusted them a second time so they'd cook crusty and crunchy in the hot, sizzling grease.

The pace quickened because I had to get all my vegetables going. Since I only had two small hands while there were three bubbling pots and a meat-filled frying pan all needing attention simultaneously, Momma, thankfully, stepped in and lent her helping hands. Otherwise, I probably would have ended up scalding myself or starting a grease fire.

The end was near… only thing left to make was the cream gravy. I flipped the chicken-fried steaks onto a platter, set the frying pan over the gas burner and announced I was ready.

Momma turned from the counter where she was busy making iced tea. "Add some flour to the pan drippings."

"How much?"

"It depends. How much grease do you have in the pan?"

"I dunno."

"Well, just eyeball it."

"Huh?"

She looked over at the pan. "Put in a handful of flour."

I grabbed a fistful and dumped it in.

"Be careful! Don't get burned. Take your spatula and stir the flour until the lumps are gone and the flour browns."

I obediently followed directions.

"Now add some milk."

"How much?"

"It depends."

"Huh?"

"It depends on how thick you want the gravy. You gotta eyeball it to get it right."

I poured from the milk carton—my hand slipped and milk splashed liberally into the skillet. Oops. "Momma, you make it."

"No," she said with a chuckle, "you're doing fine." She surveyed my work. "But keep stirring so the gravy doesn't burn."

I obliged. The gravy burped and gurgled.

She nodded and re-evaluated the process in progress. "Turn up the heat, just a smidgen."

A smidge-what? The pressure of being a sorcerer's apprentice whittled my resolve for culinary mastery. Waving my spatula in one hand and placing the other akimbo, I wailed, "Momma, this is too hard."

---

**Joyce Boatright** loves to cook and hardly ever uses a recipe. She lives and writes in Houston, Texas.

"Careful, you're slinging grease!"

Eventually the gravy made, but I was full of trepidation about future gravy making episodes—ones when my mother wasn't around. Despite the fact that mathematics and I operated in different universes, somehow I felt that I was going to master arithmetic faster than I would ever master "eyeballing." Cornered in the grips of a dilemma, I begged for a formula.

"Momma, instead of me having to eyeball this mess, you just tell me exactly how much of the stuff to put in and I'll measure it in the future."

"Can't do that, honey."

"Why not?" I might not be able to add and subtract numbers very well—especially under pressure—but I sure could figure out the angles: "What if I pour out all the pan drippings and start with an exact amount? Couldn't you give me the exact amount of flour to add, and then the exact amount of—"

She laughed. "It doesn't work that way."

It's family recipes that are handed down from mother to daughter throughout womanhood that keep the generations going, and Momma passed to me her own special directions about eyeballing, trying not to overheat when the task seems too hard, and, whenever possible, avoiding the lumps. It's funny that it has taken me forty-six years to see how much Momma's and my lives are like making gravy.

Did we learn from our mistakes? It depends. I had my share of self-made dramas, but I finally learned to go easy with the pepper, and Momma was a crusty broad when she had to be but always warm and tender beneath her thick-skinned toughness.

Did we make the right decisions as we journeyed our lives' paths? It depends. We both had our share of lumps, but we kept cookin' and the hard edges of disappointment seemed to have smoothed out over time. What can I tell you? We learned to eyeball things and make adjustments.

# Chicken-Fried Steak

### Ingredients

1 cup white flour
Salt and ground black pepper to taste (but be generous)
3 large eggs
3 tablespoons milk
4 steak cutlets (ask butcher for four generous portions of round steak that have been tenderized)
½ cup vegetable oil

### Preparation

In a shallow plate, sift together flour, salt, and pepper. In another shallow pan, combine egg and milk. Dip steaks in egg mixture, coat with flour mixture, and repeat.

In a large frying pan over medium-high heat, add vegetable oil and heat until a drop of water sizzles. Add coated steak pieces and fry 4 to 5 minutes per side or until golden brown and thoroughly cooked. Remove from pan and drain on paper towels. Keep warm until served.

Makes 4 delicious servings!

### Tips and Notes

Don't forget to serve the chicken-fried steak with cream gravy. And in case you're nervous about eyeballing it, see the recipe on page 63.

# Quebec Tourtière

**Rayn Plainfield**

My mother was a fantastic cook. Of course, what else could she be, being French Canadian? Her whole life was devoted to cooking. She surrounded herself with cookbooks. By day, when not in the garden, she could be found humming cheerily to herself, in the kitchen fragrant with cooking, flour on every surface, busily punching down bread dough or rolling out crusts for pies, while exotic sauces simmered on the stove. After dinner, her evenings were spent poring over cookbooks, ever in search of new recipes.

As a young girl, the first thing I'd ask Mom when I'd get home from school was, "What's for dinner?" and anticipate her response with bated breath! Occasionally she'd make some god-awful thing to please my father, like British curry, steak and kidney pie, or liver and onions! Yuck! But most of the time, her answer would make me swoon! I would kill time waiting impatiently for Mom's anticipated call, "Come and eat!" Dinner was the central event in our family life. Not only was it the daily event that brought us all together as a family, but because Mom was such an outstanding cook, it was most often the highlight of our day.

Dad was in the military, which means we moved every two years, so we lived all over Canada. In every single place we lived, Mom would quickly acquire renown and become downright revered for her baking and cooking. She was always generous in inviting a newly arrived military family for a home-cooked meal. People were unfailingly delighted to be invited over for the social evenings my parents hosted, as there would always be a cornucopia of baked items, both savory and sweet that Mom had spent the day creating. I would hide out in the kitchen in my pajamas on these late evenings, and Mom would sweep in from time to time from the noisy socializing in the living room with great platters of left-over pastries and encourage me to "eat all you want, my dear!" I remember mouth-watering miniature tarts filled with Mom's home-made strawberry jam, her apricot preserves and lemon curd, her spinach-cheese tarts, cream puffs, cheese-bread twists and, of course, miniature *Tourtière* tarts.

Mom often made foods that had been passed down for generations in her own family. One of our family's all-time favorites was Mom's Quebec *Tourtière*. Now, in Quebec, *Tourtière* is a popular dish, but each family has its own unique recipe. It's traditionally a meat pie, often pork but other meats can be included as well. Some families like to add vegetables. My maternal grandmother made it very simply, with onions, garlic, and the one spice that sets this dish apart—allspice. The crust is rendered heavenly by the pork fat, which infuses the pastry, so it's important

*Continues on page 88*

---

**Rayn Plainfield** was born in Canada to bicultural parents, where she grew up speaking French. She majored in Chinese and Japanese in college and studied in China and Japan for several years. Later in life Rayn returned to school, obtaining a Master's in Counseling Psychology. She married and moved to Portland, Oregon, where she now resides, making her living as a substitute teacher.

# *Quebec Tourtière*

**(Meat Pie)**

## Ingredients

### Crust

| | |
|---|---|
| 2½ | cups flour |
| ½ | teaspoon salt |
| 1 | cup lard, refrigerator-cold |
| ½ | cup ice-cold water |

### Filling

| | |
|---|---|
| 1 | pound minced pork (do not use reduced-fat pork) |
| 1 | small onion, chopped |
| 1 | or more cloves garlic, minced |
| ¼ | teaspoon salt |
| ½ | teaspoon or more ground allspice |
| ½ | cup water |
| ¼–½ | cup breadcrumbs |
| 1 | egg yolk |

## Preparation

To make the crust, mix flour and salt in a bowl. Cut lard into ¼–½-inch dice. Mix lard into the flour. Cut with a pastry cutter until the mixture is the consistency of small peas. Pour 3 tablespoons of the ice-cold water into the mixture and toss it thoroughly. Add another 2 tablespoons of water and toss again.

Pour out mixture onto a pastry board. With the heel of your hand, smear about a ¼ cup at a time away from you until the entire amount is a solid chunk of dough. Try not to overwork the dough. Gather it into a ball and chill for one hour. Then roll out 2 circles for the top and bottom pie crusts for the *Tourtière.* Use 1 circle to line the bottom of a greased 9-inch pie pan.

Place all the filling ingredients except for breadcrumbs in a saucepan. Bring to a boil, then reduce heat to simmer. Cook for 20 minutes, uncovered, over medium heat, stirring often to break up the meat. Remove from heat. Add a few spoonfuls of breadcrumbs, and let stand for 10 minutes. If the fat is not sufficiently absorbed by the breadcrumbs, add more, as needed. Cool this mixture.

Preheat the oven to 350°F.

Pour the cooled filling into the pastry-lined pie pan. Cover with pastry. Cut a small hole in the center of the pie to allow steam to escape during baking. Brush the top of the pie with beaten egg yolk.

Bake at 350°F. until the crust is golden, approximately 25–40 minutes. Allow the pie to cool a little before serving.

Serves 3–4.

### Tips and Notes

When assembling the pie, the meat portion should be no more than twice as thick as the 2 crusts combined.

*Continued from page 86*

not to use low-fat meat in this dish. Mom often served this pie with a simple salad and vinaigrette dressing. To my mother's chagrin I would eat my slice of *Tourtière* with a generous slathering of ketchup, squirted straight from the bottle! Mom always responded good-naturedly, "For heaven's sake, how can you taste anything with that much ketchup on it?" Well, you know kids!

When Mom made this dish, there was always a little extra meat left over. This was called *croton* and it's much like paté. Mom would place this leftover portion in a small bowl and refrigerate it. It made a wonderful spread over bread. I remember coming home hungry after school many a time, delighted to find some *croton* in the fridge, the day after Mom had made *Tourtière*. I'd slather a thick portion on a slab of Mom's homemade bread and practically die of happiness! When the filling was cold like this, the delicate allspice flavor was even more enhanced. This was always a great way to tide me over until supper!

I hope you'll enjoy this traditional French-Canadian meat pie as much as I have over the years since my childhood! I make a point of baking this pie every year in mid-April, the anniversary of Mom's passing, to commemorate some of our fondest memories of her.

# Irish Stew

**Pat Daly**

I learned how to use a pressure cooker from my mother-in-law. My own mother never used one in our kitchen when I was growing up in the '50s and '60s. She was afraid it would blow up, ruin her kitchen, and cause total blindness to us all. Consequently, I was very fearful of coming close to that wiggly thing that threatened to blow its top and send us all to Braille school. Well into adulthood, I wanted no part of that complicated, heavy contraption. I'd stick with Pyrex.

My mother-in-law, however, used her pressure cooker regularly and fearlessly. When I asked her to give me her recipe for Irish stew she said, "First you'll have to buy a pressure cooker." As the blood drained from my face, she laughed.

"It's the safest thing in the kitchen," she said with a wink.

The desire to replicate her delicious stew and the example of her fearless attitude won me over. Ten years ago, my family gave me a pressure cooker for Mother's Day, and I've been cooking up a storm ever since.

My mother-in-law passed away in 2001, but we celebrate her presence every time we eat Irish stew.

---

**Pat Daly** was raised in Pennsylvania and has lived in Largo, Florida, for the past twenty-one years. She works full-time as a grant writer and has a college-aged son. Pat has been a Story Circle member since 2005 and is looking forward to attending the national conference in 2008.

# *Irish Stew*

### Ingredients

- 2 pounds beef, bite-size cuts
- 2 tablespoons shortening
- 2 teaspoons salt
- ¼ teaspoon pepper
- ½ teaspoon paprika
- 1 bay leaf
- 2½ cups water
- 2 beef bouillon cubes
- 1 large onion, chopped
- 3 stalks celery, cut up
- 8 carrots, cut up
- 4 medium potatoes, quartered
- 1 29-ounce can tomatoes, whole or chopped
- 1 cup water
- ½ cup cornstarch mixed in water

### Preparation

Brown the beef in shortening in the pressure cooker, uncovered. Season with salt, pepper, paprika, and the bay leaf. Add 2½ cups water and the bouillon cubes. Cover and cook for 8–10 minutes under pressure. Cool the cooker normally for 5 minutes, then reduce the remaining pressure.

Add the vegetables and 1 cup of water. Cover and cook for 6–8 minutes. Reduce the pressure instantly (according to your cooker instructions).

Remove the meat and vegetables to a serving dish. Thicken the juices left in the pan with the cornstarch and water mixture, stirring over a medium heat to make gravy. Pour the gravy over the ingredients in the serving dish.

Serves 6–8.

### Tips and Notes

You can use London broil for this recipe. It is cheaper than "stew meat." Cut it up into bite size pieces.

This recipe is for a pressure cooker that holds 6 quarts, 15 pounds pressure.

# *Our New Year's Day Tradition*

**Donna Van Straten Remmert**

We may be the only family in America whose New Year's Day tradition is to serve sukiyaki. It started thirty-six years ago, after having had the privilege of living in Yokohama, Japan, for three years. Our two sons David and Stephen, five and six, were going through the culture shock of having just moved to Chappaqua, New York, where everything was so different from anything they could remember.

"I'd like our New Year's dinner to be the most special meal you can imagine," I said to them and my husband Jim. "What might that be?"

Without missing a beat, they all screamed, "Sukiyaki! We want Kuzuko's sukiyaki."

Kuzuko was our beloved maid, cook, interpreter, and most importantly, surrogate grandmother while in Japan, and her sukiyaki was our favorite meal. We ate it only on special occasions since Kobe beef was expensive; it's from cows that are fed lots of beer and are hand-massaged daily to ensure tenderness.

I felt up to the task since I had diligently recorded what I saw Kuzuko doing when creating her sukiyaki. And I was pleased that this would give me an excuse to use my precious antique Imari porcelain and my antique red lacquer rice bowls to serve this most special meal of the year.

To add to the excitement, my dad, who had gone through a long period of grieving my mother's untimely death, was coming from Wisconsin to introduce us to Lilas, a woman he loved and hoped to marry. Daddy had visited us in Japan, and this event would help him share his experience with Lilas.

We got a little carried away with our Japanese theme, pushing Christmas decorations to the side in order to display our new Japanese treasures and our many scrapbooks of pictures from those years. David and Stephen participated by making origami decorations for the table and elsewhere.

The event was a huge success. It even took precedence over football games on television that year. And with a few exceptions, we've continued the tradition of sukiyaki on New Year's Day. Each year, we get out the scrapbooks and spend a good portion of the day telling stories about those years. And we never fail to take pictures for Kuzuko. In many ways, this ritual is our way of honoring her. She helped us understand and love Japanese people and culture. I have never known an American who doesn't like Kuzuko's sukiyaki.

---

**Donna Van Straten Remmert** has been an active member of SCN for ten years. She has served as a Board member, facilitated workshops, and was President and Program Director for the Austin Chapter. Now in Boulder, Colorado, she facilitates a writing circle. Donna's publications include two memoirs about her childhood in the '40s and '50s, *The Littlest Big Kid* and *The Jitterbug Girl*. She is writing a third memoir about her college years, to complete her coming-of-age trilogy.

# *Kuzuko-San's Sukiyaki*

## Ingredients

### Sauce

- 1 cup Kikkoman soy sauce
- 1 cup sugar
- 1 cup water
- 2 tablespoons *mirin* (rice wine)

### Other ingredients

- 2 tablespoons olive oil
- 1 pound beef tenderloin sliced paper thin
- 2 bunches scallions, cut in 2 inch lengths; use white and green parts
- 1 block fresh hard tofu, cut in ½-inch cubes
- 6–8 large shirataki mushrooms, soaked in water overnight and sliced into bite-sized lengths
- 1 can sliced bamboo shoots
- 1 can sliced water chestnuts
- 1 large head Chinese cabbage
- Sticky rice

## Preparation

Blend all sauce ingredients in a pitcher and set aside.

Put 2 tablespoons olive oil into a large skillet and begin cooking all of the meat. After 1 minute and when meat is still a little red, add the sauce and all other ingredients, keeping each one in a separate place in the skillet (divide as in pieces of a pie). Don't overcook. It's ready to eat when the meat is brown and the veggies are still crisp.

Serve rice in a bowl and sukiyaki on a plate, again separating ingredients so each flavor can be savored to its maximum, in true Japanese style. The rice is used to cleanse the palate between bites.

Serves 6–8.

## Tips and Notes

Sukiyaki can be cooked in an electric skillet on the table. It takes 8 minutes or less.

Ask the butcher to machine cut the beef tenderloin while the beef is slightly frozen.

Dry sherry can be used instead of rice wine.

You can substitute portabella mushrooms for shirataki mushrooms.

Spinach can be substituted for Chinese cabbage.

Tofu can be omitted.

Jasmine rice can be substituted for sticky rice. Follow the directions on the package.

I serve miso soup (easy instructions are on the package) and a cucumber sesame salad with it.

The best beverage for the meal is a Japanese beer or sake (rice wine).

Dessert, in typical Japanese tradition, is honeydew melon.

# *Pinto Beans and Sopaipillas*

**Danelle Sasser**

Mom was making pinto beans in the pressure cooker. I could tell as soon as I came in from playing in the back yard because they stank up the house while they cooked, so much so that I could hardly stand to stay indoors. But I was fascinated by the pressure cooker itself. Its little hat sat on top, rocking rhythmically, saying pish-pish-pish with little bursts of steam. Mom always said, "Don't touch it!" I had images in my head of the lid blown off, stinky brown pinto bean goo all over the ceiling and walls and floor. Sadly, to me at least, that never happened. At the right time, Mom would take the pot off the burner and the pish-pish swaying of the cooker's rocker gradually slowed down. I liked it better when she put the pot in the sink and ran cold water on the lid, to bring the temperature down quicker. Sometimes she even popped off the rocker too early, causing a blast of steam to shoot up. She didn't do that for pinto beans. They needed the extra cooking time.

Even though Mom added salt, cumin, and pepper to the beans, I wouldn't eat them. I hated beans. My brother Carey loved them and, after eating his fill, would come stink up my bedroom and dash out, laughing his maniacal ten-year-old laugh when I realized what he had done. My little sister Lori, who shared the room with me, would get furious when he did this and run after him screaming. As the middle child, I was a little better at controlling myself, but I did my share of yelling at my siblings.

Fortunately for me, Mom was making more than that for dinner. We were having wine tacos and sopaipillas. I always felt mature eating wine tacos since a cup of red wine was included in the filling. Except for the wine and chili powder and the fact that the filling was served on corn tortillas softened by dipping in hot oil, this dish was a lot like sloppy joes—ground beef and tomato sauce.

We didn't have wine tacos often, so they felt special to me, a more interesting way to have the ground beef that was such a staple of many dinners. The best part of this meal was the homemade sopaipillas. Lori and I helped Mom make these. The dough was mixed with flour, baking powder, salt, and shortening, then chilled for an hour. Mom rolled the dough to just the right thickness then cut it into rough triangular shapes. Little bits of leftover dough vanished quickly into our mouths. Mom poured a huge amount of oil into a pot with high sides and heated it until it was very hot and dangerous to be near. She showed us how to slip the flat piece of dough into the hot oil without getting burned. No matter how many times I did it, I always felt the burn of hot drops of oil on my arms and hands. Then we would watch the flat dough, waiting for it to puff up. As soon as it began to swell, we had to turn it to cook the other side. With luck, we ended up with the pillowy shape of a sopaipilla.

By the time we finished frying the whole batch, we were all sweaty and red-faced and the kitchen smelled of hot oil. The reward was eating them. Mom wanted to throw out the flat ones, but they tasted fine with honey spread over them. Of course, the pillowy ones were the best. We would bite off a corner and then fill the hollow inside with way too much honey. Eating was a dripping sticky mess, but, oh, such a great combination of hot oil and dough and sweet honey—the tastes and smells of home.

# *Wine Tacos*

### Ingredients

1 pound ground beef
1 teaspoon seasoned salt
2 8-ounce cans tomato sauce
1 cup red wine or beef broth
2 teaspoons chili powder
2 tablespoons chopped green onions
8 corn tortillas
Vegetable oil (optional)
Shredded lettuce
Grated Cheddar cheese
Chopped green onion

### Preparation

Brown the ground beef and drain. Combine with seasoned salt, tomato sauce, red wine or broth, chili powder, and chopped green onions. Simmer for 15 minutes.

To soften tortillas using oil, the traditional method, pour oil into a skillet, about ½ inch deep. Heat the oil over medium heat. You are aiming for a temperature that will cause the tortilla to sizzle when it first touches the oil. Using smooth-edged tongs, dip the tortilla in the oil for a few seconds, let drip, then place onto a dinner plate. Or soften each tortilla by dipping it in the sauce for a minute or two just before placing it on the dinner plate.

Lay the tortilla flat on the dinner plate and spoon some sauce on half of the tortilla. Garnish with shredded lettuce, grated cheese and chopped green onions, and fold over the empty half of the tortilla.

Serves 4.

---

**Danelle Sasser** lives in Austin, Texas, with her husband and twin teenage boys. She spends her time taking care of her family, volunteering for several organizations, playing the flute, kayaking, reading, and occasionally writing. Her roots are in Albuquerque, New Mexico, and many of her favorite recipes come from there.

# *Comfort Me Now with Childhood Food*

**Becky Szymcik**

Some of my first memories are of sitting at the kitchen table and eating whatever my mother concocted for us that day. With seven kids, stretching the food dollars was always a priority and a challenge. Some recipes I liked, but others I dreaded, such as "everything" meatloaf, where Mom would put any and all leftovers in the ground beef, or mock "lasagna" made out of egg noodles, cottage cheese, and tomato sauce. I distinctly recall the *ick* factor of these awful meals at every age. A few times a year she would make spaghetti sauce—an all day event where the smells were fabulous and the anticipation exciting. Like many families, the kitchen was the center of our house.

I learned to cook at my mother's table and am proud to say I've become an excellent cook. I have my own meatloaf recipe that does not include leftovers, and I still make my mom's spaghetti sauce and meatballs. But my favorite dish of childhood that I love is my mom's answer to shepherd's pie. We used to call it "green-been casserole" but that name now gets competition from the Thanksgiving standard with cream of mushroom soup and French's onion rings, so I'll call it Alternative Shepherd's Pie.

For some reason, not a single one of us kids could tolerate corn mixed with ground beef. My mother began to experiment and came up with a hit: ground beef with tomato soup, green beans, and mashed potatoes. I know this doesn't necessarily sound appetizing, but it is delicious and was a huge hit with all the kids plus my dad. I've since changed the recipe slightly; I now use a can of tomato sauce instead of tomato soup. The first time I made this for my (now ex-) husband, he was convinced he would hate it and looked at it on the plate with an "Oh, gross!" college sophomore exclamation. He ate not one but two huge plates of it and it was a staple for us for years. It is a dish that brings back perfect memories of growing up in a big, loud, boisterous family and evokes all the warmth of childhood and comfort of the home I grew up in, when I need it.

Recently I've been craving this dish, and several times my plans to indulge myself have been thwarted due to things such as Friday during Lent (no meat on Fridays!) and last minute plans with friends on nights I'd planned to cook. Last week I was driving home from a meeting in another state and got stranded due to severe winter weather. It took me five hours to go twenty miles and find a hotel for the night. In the meantime, I passed dozens of accidents and had to constantly get out of the car to clear the ice off the wiper blades. At the end of the hotel driveway, my car got stuck in the snow pile made by the snowplow and it took me forty-five minutes to get my car out. I had at that point been in the car for nine hours. I was 500 feet from the hotel, which I couldn't walk to because

---

**Becky Szymcik** lives in Westborough, Massachusetts, and works for FEMA. She travels to disaster sites to help with relief efforts. Her assignment for Hurricanes Katrina and Rita prompted her joining Story Circle after she contributed a six-part series of "mini-memoirs" about her experiences to the Story Circle web page for Katrina. Becky's positive life philosophy includes the belief that world peace can be achieved through ice cream.

it was sheer ice and uphill, and I got soaked from trying to shovel the snow from around my tires. The next morning, the wiper blades came off the arms of the windshield wipers, so I had to stop at a repair shop before driving the final fifty miles homes. The ice and sleet were still coming down; the roads were passable but not great. Once I got home, my driveway hadn't been plowed, and I got stuck trying to get into the only available spot in my apartment complex. My three-hour drive home from Vermont had turned into a twenty-four-hour ordeal. I was exhausted, frazzled, stressed, and definitely had more gray hair than when I started.

I walked in my front door at noon and didn't leave my house again until it was time to go to work on Monday morning. I took a hot shower, put on my pj's, and made my alternative shepherd's pie casserole. It was exactly the remedy I needed after my ordeal. It calmed me on Saturday and restored my spirits on Sunday. I called my mother, talked to two of my sisters, emailed my brothers, sat on my couch under an Afghan made by my mother, and relished the comforts of my own home along with those memories of my youth. Sometimes, looking back is the best way to enjoy the here and now and gain strength from it, in whatever measure. And I'm certain I can handle the next winter storm or whatever other ordeal is in my future.

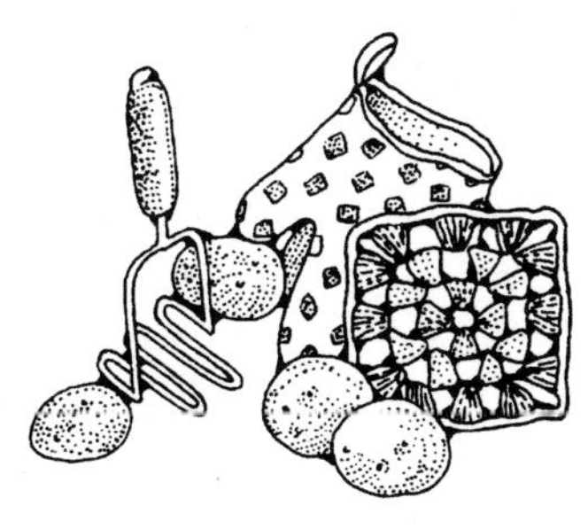

# Alternative Shepherd's Pie

### Ingredients

| | |
|---|---|
| 1 | pound ground beef |
| 1 | pound green beans |
| 1 | 15-ounce can tomato sauce |
| 3 | large baking potatoes |

### Preparation

Preheat the oven to 350°F.

Brown the ground beef and drain. Add the tomato sauce. Add salt, pepper and seasonings to taste. Cook the green beans. Peel and cook the potatoes to make mashed potatoes.

In a 2-quart casserole dish, layer the ground beef and tomato mixture in the bottom of the pan. Add the green beans and top off with mashed potatoes. Heat through for 20–30 minutes in a 350°F. oven.

Serves 4–6.

### Tips and Notes

A 10-ounce can of condensed tomato soup, no water added, can be used instead of the tomato sauce.

As a shortcut, use frozen green beans.

This recipe can easily be doubled.

# And This Is Why

**Peggie Williamson**

We were less than an hour away from our Santa Fe home and I was already bored. I had colored, played with my dolls, and counted cactus—all the way to thirty!

"How big is the ocean?" I asked again from the backseat.

"A million times bigger than your blue plastic wading pool with the yellow ducks," laughed my mom.

I could hardly wait to get to California, where we were going to the beach on our first family vacation.

"How much is a million?"

My parents groaned. This was going to be a long day.

A shiny red Chevrolet pulled out onto the highway. Neither the fourteen-year-old driver, nor his father sitting in the passenger seat, saw our approaching car. Their Chevy rammed the right side of our Buick. My mother flew out of the car, hit her head on the embankment, and was dead by day's end. She was twenty-seven years old. I was almost four.

While my father tried to put his shattered life back together, I went to live with my mother's parents. They lived in an adobe house outside of Santa Fe on forty acres of desert. They had chickens, which attracted "sneeks" that ate the eggs. My pet burro Jaco lived there too and lots of jackrabbits.

This was the fifth child my grandparents had lost. The triplets died at birth. Their son committed suicide in college. Now they had lost the last of their children, my beloved mother.

My grandmother Elizabeth was a short, round, sixty-one-year-old, with grey hair that she plastered back with "sticky-stucky" and two bobby pins. Gramma smelled faintly of White Shoulders, her favorite perfume, and she moved slowly with pain and a cane. The story goes that when she was forty-five, she "took a hard fall" and was told she would never walk again. The doctors were sure of this, and Gramma was sure they were wrong. They were wrong.

"Not quite as good as new, but I think I'll keep her." Grandpa teased.

Gramma's strong faith helped her face life's many challenges, the death of her daughter being the toughest.

When my Dad visited, I asked him, "Where did Mommy go? Mommy should be with us. I miss her," I cried. I asked other people where my mother went too, hoping to get an answer I could understand.

Despite bouts of sadness, the time with my grandparents was a happy one. There were daily visits to Grandpa in his woodworking shop where he made hand-carved furniture and sometimes a toy for me. After drawing "pictures" on the sawdust-covered floors, I'd run off to chase the jackrabbits out of Gramma's garden. It was my hardest job. I wasn't supposed to step on the plants.

"Want to help me feed and brush Jaco?" Grandpa asked as the day wound down. I had my own brush and was a

---

**Peggie Williamson,** who splits her time between Hawaii and Southern California, is the founder of *Wishworks*—a non-profit organization providing teachers in low-income schools with motivational gifts, materials and supplies. *Wishworks* in turn provides Peggie with many of the ideas for the inspirational stories she writes for newspapers and magazines. She and her husband love to cook together using fresh ingredients from their garden.

"big help." I wouldn't go near the chicken coops though; I was afraid of those sneeks. After our "hard day's work," Grandpa and I had big appetites.

"Bring in some parsley from the garden and come to dinner," Gramma would call. That green stuff "decated" every platter of food on the table.

"It's my special touch," she said, "for my special girl."

Gramma cooked my favorite meals, all named after me, of course. There was Peggy's Spaghetti, Peggy's Baked Potato Dinner, and Peggy's Pork Chops, just to name a few. After dinner there were caramels and chocolates I could eat without even asking.

Occasionally, Grandpa would take out his Swiss Army knife, signaling—a Plum Party! He'd slice up lots of plums, even ones that weren't purple. After we sampled each kind we voted on our favorite. Grandpa knew how to have fun!

Around eight-thirty, Gramma would ask, "Would you like a story, my dear girl?" Snuggled into her warm, squishy body, I drifted off to the sound of her voice, knowing I was loved and all was well.

A year passed and on a bright, Saturday morning that started out with Peggy's Pancakes my father came to visit. To our horror, he announced he was getting married. My stepmother turned out to be nothing like my mother or grandmother. There were no stories, no plums, and no parties. She cooked none of my favorite meals.

And this is why I am passionate about cooking. I cook for gatherings large and small, and you'll find each platter decorated with a fresh sprig of parsley, my "special touch." My favorite dishes to make? The ones named after me, of course.

### Ingredients

- 1 12-ounce package spaghetti
- 1 onion, chopped
- 1 green pepper, chopped
- 1 pound ground beef
- 3 10-ounce cans tomato soup
- 1 11-ounce can corn, drained
- 1 3-ounce can ripe olives, sliced
- 2 cups Cheddar cheese, grated
- Salt and pepper to taste.

### Preparation

Preheat the oven to 350°F.

Cook and drain the spaghetti.

While the spaghetti is cooking, sauté the onion and green pepper in a heavy casserole pan. Add the ground beef and brown this with the onions and green peppers; then drain.

Add the cooked spaghetti, soup, corn, olives, and cheese to the ground beef mixture in the casserole pan.

Cover the pan and cook in a 350°F. oven for 1 hour, stirring twice.

Serves 4.

# *Murdee's Stinky Goulash*

**Paula Stallings Yost**

My sassy grandmother, grandly dubbed "Murdee" by her toddler grandchild (me), loved to cook. Whenever money was short, she could make a pound of hamburger last a month. We never left the table hungry, though, no matter how far she stretched the protein. Mounds of hot, buttery mashed potatoes, sweetened white rice, or creamy noodles always complemented the entrée. Starch was cheap and cholesterol consciousness had yet to rear its ugly head.

A great believer in the boundless benefits of garlic, Murdee was convinced it kept all manner of diseases at bay, not to mention vampires. She tossed those smelly cloves into everything—meat, vegetables, bread, salad, even an especially nasty health-smoothie she whipped up daily. In the garden, garlic sprouts surrounded her tomato plants in an effort to discourage bugs and squirrels. But all that is another story. This story is about the night Murdee served her "stinky goulash" and taught me a most unusual lesson.

At the age of sixteen, a girl named Olivia and I became incredibly silly best friends. Over dinner one evening, we were chattering about our double date just an hour or so away. We were excited about seeing the latest James Bond flick at the local drive-in and, better yet, being seen in my date's flashy new 1963 Impala convertible. The only problem was that we really didn't like the boys at all. As we plotted ways to avoid sitting close to them or (heaven forbid) kissing them, Murdee chimed in. "I know just the way around that little problem. Dig into this goulash and garlic bread, eat a slice or two of that fresh onion. I'll guarantee those boys won't come anywhere near you!"

We thought that was a great idea and quickly took her advice to heart. While primping for our big night out, we expanded on the premise and sprayed ourselves with every bottle of perfume in my grandmother's vast collection, including such smoldering scents as Evening in Paris, Jungle Gardenia, and the ever-pungent Taboo. Combined, they were a nose's worst nightmare.

Our unsuspecting dates arrived on schedule and seemed suitably impressed with our appearance. Though we may have smelled to high heaven, there was no way we would go out in public looking anything short of glamorous. The young men's ardor noticeably cooled, however, as we glided past them through the front door. Exchanging stunned glances, they were more than happy to allow us ample space in the car. They must have been grateful, too, that they had lowered the convertible's ragtop earlier.

Murdee's scheme worked extremely well. Those boys kept a respectable distance throughout the movie and even made several prolonged trips to the concession stand for popcorn, sour pickles, and Dr. Peppers. They made a lot of treks to the bathroom, too. Maybe it was all those Dr. Peppers. Olivia and I had a blast, snickering every time they found a new reason to leave.

---

An award-winning memoirist and personal historian, **Paula Stallings Yost** believes passionately in the power of story. In 1999, she jettisoned a twenty-five-year public relations/journalism career along with life in the suburbs to found *LifeSketches/Heirloom Memoirs*—a biography service based in the piney woods of East Texas. Helping others preserve their family histories (real stories of people from all walks of life) has become the perfect niche for her talents and expertise. Paula's website is www.alifesketch.com.

By the end of the evening, our dates were mumbling something about early curfews as we pulled into my grandmother's driveway. Each boy chivalrously leaned across the seat to open our car doors with the engine still running.

"We were absolutely right about those two, Olivia," I whispered as we entered the house. "Real gentlemen would have walked us to the door."

My grandmother popped up from the living-room sofa at that moment, anxious to hear all about our non-amorous adventures. Soon we were sharing the details of our strange night out, and she began to giggle uncontrollably. Wiping tears of glee from her cheeks, Murdee finally declared, "See? I told you it'd work," and marched merrily off to bed to relate our story to her husband. It was a long time before their muffled laughter died down that night.

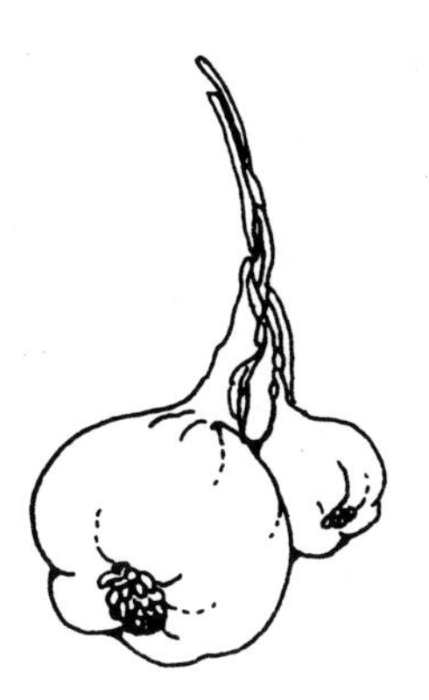

## Murdee's Stinky Goulash

### Ingredients

- 1 pound ground beef
- 6 garlic cloves, minced
- 1 onion, diced
- 6 cups water
- 2 tablespoons ketchup
- 1 10-ounce can tomato soup
- 1 pound package elbow macaroni
- 1 bay leaf
- 1 teaspoon oregano, chopped
- Dash cayenne pepper
- Salt and pepper to taste
- Parmesan cheese

### Preparation

Brown the beef, garlic, and onion together in a deep, heavy pan. Drain. Add the water, ketchup, and tomato soup and bring to a boil. Add the macaroni, bay leaf, oregano, salt, and pepper and return to a boil.

Reduce heat, cover and simmer for about 25 minutes, stirring occasionally.

Sprinkle Parmesan cheese atop each serving.

Serves 4.

# The Power of Memory

**Anne Beckner**

My father ran a small bakery when I was a child growing up on the west coast of Florida. I loved to visit and get pie scraps to snack on and watch the big mixers turning out dough for bread. My father was an excellent cook and one of his favorite things to do with ham was to encase it in bread dough and bake it in one of the great ovens with circulating shelves along with the bread loaves for the next day. He baked it for an indeterminate length of time and it was very dark when he removed it. He intended to crack the crust off and discard it, but I would stand by to retrieve the shards of crisp bread with its succulent broth-soaked interior to gobble up. The power of memory is so strong; I can almost taste it today.

# Ham Baked in Bread Dough

**Ingredients**

| | |
|---|---|
| 4 | cups all-purpose flour |
| 1½ | teaspoons salt |
| 3 | packages dry yeast |
| 1⅓ | cups warm water |
| 1 | 6- or 7-pound ham |

**Preparation**

Combine the flour and the salt. Dissolve the yeast in the warm water and pour into the dry ingredients. Stir until it is well combined and it becomes an elastic, even dough. Cover the dough and let it rise in a warm place for 1 hour. It should double in size.

Turn the dough out onto a floured work surface and use a rolling pin to roll it out to ½-inch thickness. The dough may be an irregular shape. Place the ham in the middle of the dough and completely wrap it in the dough. Pinch the edges together to seal. Place the ham on a baking sheet and let it sit for 20 minutes.

In a preheated oven, bake the ham for 2 hours at 350°F. after which time the crust should be light golden and fragrant. Slice and serve.

Serves 8–10.

---

**Anne Beckner** has always loved to cook and comes from a long line of good cooks who taught her a lot. The happy result is that her grown children all have a keen interest in good food and cooking. Even her six-year-old grandson has been eating brie and Greek olives since he was an infant. Anne likes to read cookbooks, especially regional ones, and to experiment with new recipes.

# Cookies and Cakes

# *Fresh Cold Milk*

**Rachael Hungerford**

The milkman left four quarts of whole milk in the box on our front porch every other day but Sunday. He came and went very early in the morning, stopping to give a gentle pat and a quick word to the black cat who sat purring on the porch railing. Dad brought the milk into the house as soon as he got up. If it was left outside too long, even in the insulated box made for it, the milk soured in the summer heat, smelling up the whole porch, or froze in the winter cold, popping the cap like a small erupting volcano.

Fresh milk was a treasure to my family. For us, the years of the Great Depression meant there had been little work and seldom enough money to buy fresh vegetables, meat, or milk. Then, World War II rationing meant we could only buy so much fresh milk and never enough at any one time. When finally the war and rationing ended and there was enough money, fresh milk became a priority and was a part of every meal and a treat our family enjoyed.

Those slices of hot homemade bread, fresh from the oven with butter melting into all the nooks and crannies, needed big glasses of fresh cold milk to wash them down. Grandma's freshly-made molasses cookies, round and dense with spices and a bit of sugar sprinkled on top and served with fresh cold milk, made Sunday evenings worth waiting for. Thick, yellow cream, carefully poured off the top of a bottle of fresh cold milk, was swirled through my mother's first cup of coffee every morning. Golden-yellow noodles, slippery with butter, salt, and pepper and accompanied by fresh cold milk, made the walk home from school for lunch worthwhile for me. After school, a couple of sandwiches and a quart of fresh cold milk drunk straight from the bottle kept my brother going until supper. My father's bedtime snack was Saltine crackers crushed in a bowl, covered with fresh cold milk, and eaten with a spoon. Best of all were the huge, sweet, red, ripe strawberries, sliced in half, piled into a bowl and covered with sugar and fresh cold milk—an afternoon snack or dessert anytime and as much as any of us wanted.

Fresh cold milk is still part of every meal and every treat I prepare. It's the best treasure in my kitchen. I am thankful, always, for its comfort and the everyday memories it brings back to me.

---

**Rachael Hungerford** is a college professor in a small liberal arts college in a small town in Pennsylvania. She teaches education methods courses and women's studies courses. She has three children and four grandchildren and loves them all. She hosts a women's writing group once a week. It's been meeting for three years! She'll do more of this when she retires. Books and writing are her passion.

# *Grandma Lilly's Molasses Cookies*

### Ingredients

| | |
|---|---|
| 6 | cups sifted flour |
| 1 | cup sugar |
| 1 | cup shortening |
| 1 | tablespoon ground cinnamon |
| 1 | teaspoon ground cloves |
| 1 | teaspoon ground ginger |
| 2 | eggs |
| 1 | cup molasses |
| 4 | level teaspoons baking soda |
| 6 | tablespoons sour milk |

### Preparation

Preheat oven to 350°F.

Sift 6 cups of flour into a large bowl and set aside. Cream the sugar and shortening together. Add the spices to this mixture. Add the eggs and beat the batter until smooth.

In a separate small bowl, add the baking soda to the molasses and beat until foamy. Add the molasses mixture to the sugar and shortening mixture. Add the sour milk to this mixture.

Gradually add the flour until the dough is soft and easy to handle. It will be just a bit sticky. Roll out the dough and cut out with cookie cutters. Sprinkle each cookie with a pinch of sugar. Bake at 350°F. for 10–12 minutes.

Makes at least 5-dozen cookies.

### Tips and Notes

To sour regular milk, add a few drops of vinegar.

If you prefer, you may refrigerate the dough for an hour to make it easier to handle but this is not absolutely necessary.

# Cinderella Cookies

**Susan Ideus**

I knew Christmas would be different this year. Though my mother and I had not been close, her August death would impact all of us. Our daughters had never known a holiday without their Gram, and my mother had been a part of my life every Christmas, even when I had lived in places too distant to travel home every year. We determined to make this a happy time, and we were especially glad to hear that my twin brother Jim would be spending a few days with us over the holidays. He is single and lives alone, and much of his free time over the years had been spent tending to Mother's everyday needs. I had been with her for extended periods of time over the past year as she dealt with her final illness. My brother and I would both be dealing with her loss, and I wasn't exactly sure what memories might come to the fore over the next few days.

Becca and Johanna chopped down *the* perfect Christmas tree. Then we cleaned and cooked and cleaned and cooked and decorated and cleaned—emphasis on *clean*—to impress my twin, who was a neatnik from way back while I tended to be just the opposite. The girls thought it was hilarious when I told them the story of Jim's cleaning my room for me when we were young teens, just so I wouldn't get grounded. I'm sure he exacted a price for that, though details escape me.

The day before Jim's arrival, I looked around and thought it all looked good enough to meet with even Mr. Clean's approval. The decorations and a lovely tree were in place, and we had food enough for several families. Still, at the last minute, I decided to make just one more batch of cookies, an old family recipe and my brother's favorite, a buttery date cookie called Cinderella Cookies, origin of strange name unknown.

I gathered all the ingredients and measured, chopped, and diced according to the recipe. I'd helped Mom with these cookies numerous times over the years, so I was sure this would be no trouble and would be a special treat for Jim. The girls were occupied elsewhere, and my husband was watching TV, so it was just me and the dates and nuts in the kitchen. I mixed everything together, and there was my cookie dough—a gooey, gelatinous mess! This wouldn't make cookies; it looked more like a thick batter. I needed help and the only other person with the recipe was my mother. And then, it hit me—I couldn't just pick up the phone and call her to ask what I'd done wrong.

Two days before Christmas, I stood in the middle of our kitchen with a bowl of cookie goop, crying as I had not even when she died. It must have been a keening, pitiful cry, because both girls and Harold came running. One of them took the bowl, and they all gathered around, hugging me until the crying abated enough for me to speak.

"I can't ever call my mother again," was all I managed to choke out.

---

**Susan Ideus,** an Internet Chapter member since January 2006, lives in Magnolia, Texas, with Harold, her husband of thirty-eight years, and their Cairn Terrier, Duffy. Susan and Harold have two lovely daughters, Rebecca and Johanna, who live nearby. Susan's hobbies are reading, needlework, and, her real passion, writing, and she is doing memoir work at the urging of her daughters. Her current dream is to retire and write whenever and wherever she might be, since traveling RV-style through this wonderful country of ours is also part of that dream.

No matter what our relationship had been or what I might have wished it was, I learned something that day. There are just times when a girl needs her mother. I'd never had much of mine, and that made the grieving deeper. I did miss her, but it was so much more. There was grief for her life, which seemed to hold so little joy for her, and grief for all it could have been. I mourned the relationship we never had and the one I had always longed for. I grieved all the unknown possibilities of her and me together. That would be with me for some time to come.

There were to be no answers for me that day concerning my mother. The cookies, thankfully, were another story. A few hours in the refrigerator and that dough made the best batch of Cinderella cookies ever, and I decided the "magic" transformation of the dough might account for their name. Even better was the big hug I got from my brother. You know, I just remembered—all those years ago, when he cleaned my room, I baked him a batch of cookies!

# Cinderella Icebox Date Cookies

### Ingredients

- 2 cups brown sugar
- 2 cups granulated sugar
- 2 cups butter, melted
- 6 eggs
- 7 cups flour
- 2 teaspoons baking soda
- 2 cups chopped dates
- 2 teaspoons vanilla

### Preparation

Mix the sugars and the butter in a large bowl. Beat in the eggs, one at a time. Add the other ingredients. The dough will be soft. Shape the dough into rolls or logs. Wrap it well and chill at least overnight.

Slice the dough into ¼-inch rounds and bake in a moderate (350–375°F.) oven until golden brown.

Makes approximately 6-dozen cookies.

### Tips and Notes

The cookies should be soft enough to be chewy, so don't overcook.

# *Keeping the Christmas Spirit— At All Costs*

**Lisa Shirah-Hiers**

Recently I ran across a book about Christmas in Denmark. Glancing at it idly as I re-shelved books in my daughter's school library, I was astonished to read that the cookie-baking frenzy that is such a part of my childhood isn't just a quirk of my family. It stems from an ancient Danish superstition: if a guest wasn't offered sweets, they'd steal away the Christmas spirit when they left.

Now, I knew the Danish and German origins of our family's opinion that fewer than seven varieties of cookies at Christmas is, well, lazy. What I didn't realize is how serious this baking business is. It's only marginally comforting that my ancestresses on both sides of the Atlantic have suffered the cookie crunch year after year. Because, of course, you can't make them too far ahead. They'd go stale. So year in, year out, I slave to produce a bakery's worth of sweet joy, which my family of three can't possibly eat but without which the holidays simply wouldn't be the same.

Of course I could choose to bake less. We've altered other family traditions with nary a backward glance. But this isn't just tradition. It's sacred. And anyway—what about that whole Christmas spirit thing? Somehow Christmas wouldn't be Christmas without toffee bars, gingersnaps, butterballs, peppermint meringues, raspberry bars, red and green sugar cut-outs, mini cheesecake tarts, pecan tarts, date bars, fudge, cookie press, Hershey's Kisses, and Oma's oatmeal cookies. Why, the plate just wouldn't look right. And that, of course, is what it's all about. The cookie plate.

Mine is two-tiered. And it's big. It has to be. I'm sure if I tried to fill it with store-bought delicacies, it would crack in two. Like my ancestresses' hearts. And two or three or five varieties just look too bare. Too bland. Too boring. Too colorless. No. A good cookie platter must bloom in every shade and hue like a well-tended garden.

I have never compromised on the cookie issue. Not in years I was on a diet, not in years we were leaving anyway, not in years we barely had enough money for Christmas dinner—not even in our first few years of marriage when the kitchen counter was only slightly larger than the cookie sheet. I cried, but I didn't compromise.

I know there are females in the family not cursed with the cookie gene, or at least those with a milder case. But I and my poor aunt—who sometimes bakes three or four batches of the same cookie because her family actually *eats* them—we are doomed.

So please. When you remember the less-fortunate this season, keep us in your thoughts and prayers. And if you can find it in your heart, send flour. Lots and lots of flour.

---

**Lisa Shirah-Hiers** is a piano teacher, free lance writer and writing workshop facilitator in Austin, Texas. She has published several articles in the *Hill Country Sun*, *austinwoman* and *Austin Monthly* magazine and an essay in *What Wildness Is This: Women Write about the Southwest* and serves on the Story Circle Network board. She is married to Scott Hiers, a very patient hydrologist with whom she has one curious, brilliant eight-year-old daughter.

# *Oma's Gingersnaps*

## Ingredients

### Creamed ingredients

- 1 cup lard (yes...lard)
- ½ cup butter
- 1 cup molasses (dark, but not blackstrap)
- 2 cups white sugar

### Ground Spices

- 2 teaspoons ginger
- 2 teaspoons cinnamon
- ½ teaspoon nutmeg
- ¼ teaspoon cloves
- ¼ teaspoon allspice

### Remaining ingredients

- 7 cups white flour (1 cup reserved for rolling)
- 1 cup buttermilk
- 1 teaspoon baking soda in about ¼ cup hot water
- ½ teaspoon salt

## Preparation

Mix the creamed ingredients (lard, butter, molasses and sugar). Add the spices. Add 6 cups or so of the flour, as well as the buttermilk, the baking soda dissolved in hot water, and the salt. The remaining flour will be used when you roll the dough out. Refrigerate the dough overnight.

Roll the dough out in manageable amounts and cut it with cookie cutters. This is a very, very soft dough. It will take a "light touch, patience, and perseverance." It is usually the second rolling out before a batch can be cut and lifted.

Work in the flour as needed. The less you work in, the crisper and tenderer the cookies will be. Too much flour makes thick, hard, less flavorful cookies.

Bake the cookies for about 10 minutes at 350–375°F. Bake them 5 minutes on the lower oven shelf, then 5 minutes on the upper shelf. Watch! The thinner you roll them, the more easily they will burn.

Makes about 14-dozen cookies.

## Tips and Notes

My family has preserved this gingersnap recipe that was brought from Germany by my great-grandmother in the 1800s. The original copy says that it "makes about 10,000 cookies." According to Aunt Susie, her mother, **my** Oma, always said that by the time you finished standing there rolling out all the cookies, you felt like you were standing on "bloody stumps" and had been at it forever.

Aunt Susie says you can cut the recipe in half successfully, but I say, why risk running out of cookies and angering the Christmas Spirit?

# *Springerle: A Christmas Tradition*

**Lavon Urbonas**

Traditions are the colorful ribbons that keep the box of eclectic holiday memories intact. Since my children were young, I have hosted a family Christmas Eve at our home. This evolved from the tradition of my own youth when relatives would gather at Aunt Ann and Uncle Raymond's home.

The food that remains a tradition from that era is Springerle—Swiss picture cookies, piquant with anise seeds. Aunt Ann made them then. When we moved and no longer went "over the freeway and through the 'hoods" to be with those relatives on Christmas Eve, we were without Springerle for our own celebration. That is, until Aunt Martha began to mail a batch from Michigan each year, accompanied by written instructions to "store with a slice of bread in an airtight container" to keep them soft. For twenty-five years, the Springerle arrived soon after Thanksgiving. They were so carefully packaged that only a couple were broken. Those, of course, had to be eaten immediately upon opening the box and basking in the nostalgic licorice-like aroma.

Family members looked forward to the pillowy little delights, straw colored and slightly crunchy on the outside, cream colored and soft on the inside. My mother especially enjoyed the pictures and carefully picked out her favorites among the most perfect of the specimens to give to her friends. I've always liked both eating and looking at them, but I didn't truly appreciate what a gift of love Aunt Martha had been sending us until the year she mailed the Springerle forms along with the cookies. She was, she explained at eighty years of age, getting too old to make them. Her only child, my cousin Joe, would not be the one to carry on the tradition.

My first attempt at making Springerle was a solo learning process. There are lessons that can't be learned from a typed recipe; I wish Aunt Martha had been by my side. First, I learned why she had decided to pass this torch. The process "from scratch to batch" takes two days and is labor-intensive. It also requires muscle and intuition. After two or three years, I learned how much flour was needed for dough of just the right consistency; it can't be too stiff to roll out nor so soft that it sticks to the forms. The weather is a factor, too. High humidity causes the dough to be stickier, and the cookies will not dry as thoroughly overnight before baking the next day.

When my granddaughter was ten, she became my assistant. Julie is twenty-two now. Over the years we've become proficient at determining just when the egg-and-powdered-sugar mixture is "thick and lemon colored," and when the dough feels malleable. We noticed that the cookies in the center of the baking sheet were not baking through, so we began leaving the center empty. We've even gotten creative and made some non-traditional Springerle with almond flavoring and sesame seeds in place of anise oil and anise seeds. This yummy time together is spiced with family stories and giggles and talk of school, boyfriends, hopes, and dreams.

New traditions evolve from the old; it's the natural order of life. I have passed the hosting of Christmas Eve to the next generation, just as one day I'll pass the Springerle molds along to Julie when I am too old to stir the dough.

Meantime, I am holding tight to my box of holiday memories.

# Springerle

### Ingredients

| | |
|---|---|
| 4 | large eggs |
| 1 | pound powdered sugar, sifted |
| 20 | drops (½ teaspoon) anise oil |
| 3¾ | cups all purpose flour (or more) |
| 1 | teaspoon baking powder |
| | Anise seed |

### Preparation

With an electric mixer, beat the eggs until light. Gradually add the sugar and continue beating on high speed for 15 minutes or until batter is thick and lemon colored. Add the anise oil.

Sift the flour and baking powder together. Blend into the egg mixture on low speed, ending by using a spoon to mix. Cover the batter with waxed paper or foil and let it stand at least 15 minutes in the fridge until cold.

Roll the dough about ¼ inch thick on a lightly floured surface. Let it stand for a few minutes. Press the Springerle forms firmly into the dough. Cut the cookies apart and place them on a lightly floured surface. Let them stand overnight, uncovered and exposed to the air.

Preheat the oven to 300°F.

Grease a cookie sheet. Rub the underside of each cookie with water and dip it into the anise seed. Place them on the cookie sheet. Bake at 300°F. for 15–20 minutes or until straw colored.

Makes about 5-dozen cookies.

### Tips and Notes

Aunt Martha's note: "I do not beat the mixture for 15 minutes. That was probably for when you beat by hand. I do it 'by heck and by gosh.'

"There is no single shape for the Springerle form. The most traditional is probably the rolling pin. Of the flat forms, many are made of wood. Mine are made of some kind of metal. Some newer ones are plastic. Some of the flat forms make a single cookie; mine make a dozen, with each cookie design being different."

If you do not have forms: after rolling out the cookie dough, simply cut the dough into whatever shape and size you might want (rectangular, square) or use biscuit or cookie cutters.

---

**Lavon Urbonas** was used to writing about food as a Registered Dietitian, but she's finding it a lot more fun now that she's retired and creative writing has become her hobby. Everyday events inspire short stories, poems, and memoirs. She is proud that several of her stories (no, not all about food) have appeared in the *Story Circle Journal*.

# Crater Tar Cookies

**Sharon Blumberg**

When I was a teenager, around the age of thirteen in 1970, my mother, now sadly deceased, and I were quite close. Oftentimes it seemed as if we were girlfriends, in addition to being mother and daughter. In fact, our whole family has always been very close with one another. Whenever my sister, who was almost two years older than I, had the whim, she would whip up a batch of the most luscious chocolate brownies from a family recipe. Once out of the oven, they did not last too long in our household. When this treat was ready for our indulgence, we would cut squares from the center of the pan outward. We enjoyed devouring the warm, gooey mixture while it was still hot.

One summer afternoon, my sister had just finished baking a pan of these brownies, but the ringing phone brought her some last minute plans to go out with friends for a few hours.

"Don't eat these until I come back; then we can all eat them together," she told us.

"Okay, but don't be too long," we retorted back in disgust.

Shortly after my sister left, my mother and I could not control our impulses as we sat inhaling the aroma of the chocolate treasure. First, we took just a small sample. Then, little by little, before we realized it, we had left our guilty calling card directly in the middle of the pan!

My mother and I started to laugh as we pondered what to do next. To complicate matters even more, since we were a family that could put on pounds easily, we felt even more guilty about ingesting the additional, rich calories. Suddenly, we came up with the perfect plan to cover our tracks. Since we lived about twenty minutes walking distance from the Jewel Grocery, we walked to the store in order to burn up the calories of our "crime." We bought the ingredients for a new batch of brownies and whipped them up before my sister's arrival back home.

The plan turned out just fine. We all enjoyed the treat after she came back home later that afternoon. But my mom and I enjoyed it a little less due to our previous chocolate binge. Years later, my mother and I would often laugh as we recounted the events of that day.

About twelve years later, after I got married, my husband's grandfather would enjoy these brownies whenever we dined together. He was from eastern Europe, and in his endearing thick accent, he would refer to them as "Tar Cookies." He would eat one after another as he marveled over how they cured his heartburn!

---

**Sharon Blumberg** resides in Munster, Indiana, with her husband and dog. She has a daughter who recently graduated from college and a son who is in his second year of college. She has been a Spanish teacher for the last twelve years at Parker Junior High in Flossmoor, Illinois. In her spare time, she is aspiring to see her second career, as a freelance writer, flourish.

# Double Chocolate Brownies

## Ingredients

| | |
|---|---|
| ¾ | cup flour, unsifted |
| ¼ | teaspoon baking soda |
| ¼ | teaspoon salt |
| ⅓ | cup butter |
| ¾ | cup sugar |
| 2 | teaspoons water |
| 2 | cups semi-sweet real chocolate morsels, divided |
| 1 | teaspoon vanilla extract |
| 2 | eggs |
| ½ | cup nuts, chopped |

## Preparation

Preheat the oven to 325°F.

In a small bowl, combine the flour, baking soda, and salt; set the mixture aside.

In a small saucepan, combine the butter, sugar, and water; bring the mixture just to a boil. Remove the saucepan from the heat. Add 1 cup of the chocolate morsels and the vanilla extract. Stir the mixture until the morsels melt and the mixture is smooth. Transfer the mixture to a large bowl.

Add the eggs, one at a time, beating well after each addition. Gradually blend in the flour mixture. Stir in the remaining 1 cup of the chocolate morsels and the nuts. Spread the batter into a greased 9-inch square baking pan. Bake at 325°F. for 30 minutes. Cut into 2¼-inch squares.

Makes 16 squares.

**Susan Myrick**

I press my nose against the window of memory. I peer through and replay the Christmases of my childhood.

Christmas Eve dinner, early and rushed, is an overwrought affair. Mother, frenzied after the day's chores, is irritable and unhappy with us, her three children. My stepfather Bill, unhappy over Mother's unhappiness, is even more irritable with us. There are someone's tears, another's whining, poor appetites, and always, spilled milk. Kitchen and living room clean up are essential before tempers improve. Our deep red carpet, an attractive but impractical choice of décor, demands frantic last-minute attention. The grandparents soon will gather at our house.

After dinner, my two younger sisters and I slip into hand-made dresses that Mother has made with care. Our hair gleams from her afternoon scrubbings. Once we are transformed into Christmas princesses, cacophony ends: princesses do not bicker. Radiant in red velvet, lace, and black patent leather, we step onto the Christmas Eve stage.

We pull on our good wool coats; if lucky, we will need our snow boots. We hustle into the big—I mean big—'50s era Oldsmobile. Our drive takes us through nearby neighborhoods, starry with Christmas lights. My younger sisters, breathless as violins, believe that while our horseless carriage drives us through the jeweled streets, Santa is at our house leaving presents.

Upon return, we find our house aglow with light and our grandparents' cars parked along the curb. Inside, red and gold crackle from the fireplace, dance across the walls, and twirl through the air. The spaces under and spreading from the tree are gorged with wrapped gifts. Four grandparents, playing innocent, wait for us in the living room, wearing their Christmas best.

The house sings with greetings, the rustle of dresses, and the click of high heels. The gathering is electric with expectation, the house snug with abundance. Adult bodies bend in laughter. Glitter jumps from the tree. Foil slivers on the tree sway and jump to snap at playful hands when my little sisters slide their shoes along the red carpet. The scene repeats itself in glassy reflections at the windows, as if it had more to tell. We become our own orchestra, sounding hymns in praise of high spirits.

"More presents this year than last!" someone always exclaims.

"More this year than ever!" Shaking of heads in disbelief and amazement affirms agreement all around.

Grandmother and Granddad's antique egg basket, the one they will fill with their gifts, sits against the wall near the front door. Mamma and Pa's basket sits against a wall in the kitchen. The women's best perfumes mingle with the aromas of treats that cover the kitchen table: Grandmother's apple kuchen, Mother's dark fruitcake, and Mamma's Boston brown bread, the spread completed by each cook's best cookies.

---

**Susan Myrick** lives in suburban Chicago with her husband, an inventor and lawyer, in a house on the village historical registry. Built in 1877, the house stimulates her interest in memory and history. Before retirement, she taught high school science, photography, and cooking. She is a mother of two and a new grandmother. As well as the *Story Circle Journal*, her memoirs have appeared in the Northwestern University *OLLI Journal* and in an anthology, *Gifts from Our Grandmothers*.

# Mamma Winnie's Apple Kuchen

### Dough Ingredients

- 1 cup milk
- ½ cup sugar
- 1 teaspoon salt
- ½ cup margarine
- ¼ cup warm water
- 1 package dry yeast
- 1 egg, beaten
- 4–4½ cups flour

### Topping Ingredients

- 2 medium apples
- ½ cup sugar
- ½ teaspoon ground cinnamon
- 2 tablespoons melted butter

### Preparation

Scald the milk. Stir in the sugar, salt, and margarine. Allow the mixture to cool to lukewarm. Measure the warm water into a large warm bowl; sprinkle in the yeast and stir until dissolved.

Stir together the milk mixture, the yeast mixture, the egg, and half the flour. Beat until smooth. Add the remaining flour to make a stiff batter. Cover loosely with aluminum foil; refrigerate at least 2 hours.

Pat half the dough into a greased 13x9x2-inch jelly-roll pan, pushing dough up the pan sides to form a ridge.

Pare and slice the apples thinly. Arrange the apple slices in rows on top of the dough, slightly overlapping. Mix the sugar and cinnamon and sprinkle it on the apples. Drizzle the top with 2 tablespoons of melted butter. Cover with a cloth and let rise until doubled, about an hour. Bake at 375°F. for about 35 minutes.

Makes 24 squares.

### Tips and Notes

The unbaked dough may be kept in the refrigerator up to 3 days.

---

Soon everyone begins to settle into living room chairs for the night's main activity. My stepfather's red vest is the sign of his role as gift distributor. He strolls to the tree to choose one gift from among the spread. One gift at a time is handed out and opened before the attentive admiring audience.

Everyone takes a turn displaying pleasure, oohing at the gift receiver, ahhing at the giver. Meanwhile, the object of the receiver is to be pleased, no matter what. Favorite gifts are treasured and remembered. Disappointments cannot touch us this night.

When the unwrapping ends, we head to the kitchen for coffee, dessert, and small glasses of an awful tasting wine called sherry. "Whaddya do to that cake this year? Never tasted so good!"

Grandparents linger at the front door, holding their baskets of opened gifts: lacy petticoats, leather gloves, silk stockings, new hammers, and yet another bottle of that wine—loot like no other year before. Sighs, thank you, and thank you again.

"Wasn't it a wonderful Christmas?"

"Never had one this nice. We'll never top tonight!"

# A Taste of Wonder: Wacky Cake

**Melinda Sherman**

Cooking was a practical necessity in my family during the 1950s and '60s. Except for holidays and birthdays, meals were simple and concocted from what was on hand, in season, and inexpensive. On ordinary days, Mom delighted in preparing desserts. She had a sweet tooth, and it showed in her baking. It defies reason to look back and know that we ate a diet heavy to bursting with fat and carbs like red meat, sausages, potatoes, and gravy, and with very little in the way of fresh produce. Nearly every dinner was topped off with a great dessert. Yet none of us were ever seriously overweight. I fight the battle of the bulge today knowing all about good nutrition and the availability of fresh foods and healthy frozen meals, and I wonder: How did we do it?

I'll never forget the moment when the kitchen became a place of wonderment and mystery. I'd been doing dishes for a penny a night starting at the age of four, so by the age of ten, kitchen duty had become a chore. My fresh outlook came on a day when I was passing through the kitchen on my way out the back door. Mom said, "Mitzi, come here. Watch this." She was making a cake. She stood over a mixing bowl with a mound of dry ingredients.

"I'm going to make three dents in this mountain with my spoon, see?" she said as she pressed her wooden spoon into the soft heap and made caves. "Now watch what happens!" She measured vinegar, melted shortening, and baking soda into the three indentations. She watched the batter expectantly. A frothing, gently hissing explosion of bubbles erupted as the ingredients mixed and the batter came alive.

"Isn't that something? This is a wacky cake," Mom went on to say. "No eggs."

All I knew up to that point was that a wacky cake is delicious. I especially liked the thick tan frosting. The caramel flavor seemed to make the chocolate taste even richer. Mmm—I can picture it now, a fork snapping through the hard fudge frosting and gliding through the moist black cake.

Mom always baked her cake in a thirteen by nine inch metal pan, and she kept it fresh with a lid that slid on top of the pan. She took it to countless picnics and family gatherings as well as making it at home, just for us. Her favorite season to enjoy it was autumn.

"Doesn't this crisp autumn weather make your mouth water for a wacky cake?" she said last fall, at the age of eighty-eight.

---

**Melinda Sherman** was born and raised in Ohio. After college she moved to New York City, enjoyed a career in publishing, and got married. She now lives on Long Island, where she works as a facilitator of Taproot Writing Workshops and as an Adult Education teacher of English as a second language. Melinda is an avid journal and memoir writer.

# Wacky Cake

**(Chocolate Cake)**

### Ingredients

| | |
|---|---|
| 3 | cups flour |
| 2 | cups sugar |
| 6 | tablespoons cocoa |
| 1 | teaspoon salt |
| 10 | tablespoons melted shortening |
| 2 | teaspoons baking soda |
| 2 | teaspoons white vinegar |
| 2 | cups water |
| 2 | teaspoons vanilla |

### Preparation

Preheat oven to 350°F. Grease and flour a 13x9-inch cake pan.

Sift together the first four ingredients into a large bowl. Make 3 indentations in the mixture. Pour the melted shortening into one indentation, the baking soda into the second, and the vinegar into the third. Pour 2 cups of water on top of the mountain. Mix the batter. Stir in the vanilla. Pour into a pan.

Bake for 30–35 minutes. Allow to cool.

Makes one 13x9-inch cake.

# Tan Fudge Frosting

### Ingredients

| | |
|---|---|
| 2 | cups light brown sugar |
| ½ | cup milk |
| ½ | cup cream |
| 1 | teaspoon vanilla |

### Preparation

Place sugar, milk, and cream in a heavy skillet over moderate heat. Bring to a boil. Stir constantly until the mixture reaches a "soft boil," when a drop or two sticks together in a cup of water. This usually takes 10 to 15 minutes. Remove it from the heat and cool slightly. Beat in the vanilla. Then immediately frost the cake. (The fudge frosting will harden in the pan if you wait too long.)

### Tips and Notes

Use 1 cup Half and Half instead of cream and milk, if desired.

# *My Cookbook*

**Tricia Stephens**

Picking up my favorite cookbook to make a cinnamon coffee cake, my mind flashes back over thirty years to Mom's smile as I look through the book for the first time.

I remember I didn't think I needed a cookbook, even though I was getting married, moving out, and had limited cooking experience. I had the idea my skills would magically improve once I was in my own kitchen.

At first cooking dinner seemed pretty easy. Often my husband would grill meat and I'd bake potatoes and make a salad. Sometimes I'd bake chicken, other times spaghetti with mushrooms and butter would be dinner.

Within a few months I was tired of eating the same meals, but I didn't want to admit to family and friends that I needed help, so I got out my cookbook and starting reading. The first dish I decided to prepare was fried okra. It sounded so good, so different from our usual baked potato. I set everything out on the counter and heated up a big skillet of oil. I cut up okra, dipped it in batter and rolled it in corn meal. Then I fried it until golden brown; it looked great.

My husband was the first to try a bite, and "try" was as far as he got; my beautiful okra was rock hard. The fork didn't penetrate it, instead it shot off the plate, and the next couple of pieces followed along. I burst into tears as I watched our cat chase the okra pellets across the floor.

The next day I got my cookbook back out; I wasn't going to give up. Each week I'd pick a different recipe: an entree, vegetable, or dessert. Within six months my cookbook had a large circular burn on the front cover where I'd accidentally set it on fire, several pages were wrinkled from being washed, and many pages looked like my college textbooks with notes and memos in the margins.

Over the years I've received some great cookbooks; I collect all kinds. I like the ones with straightforward, practical recipes for days we don't want to spend a lot of time in the kitchen. I like the ones with salads and no cooking involved for the really hot time of the summer in Texas when just thinking about turning on the oven causes me to break into a sweat. I like the ones that take a lot of preparation for lazy Sunday afternoons. Sometimes the list of ingredients takes my family on a treasure hunt that ends in finding a grocery store we didn't know about. Sometimes we've planted another herb in our garden so we can say, "We grew this ourselves."

I learned that cooking flows over into all parts of my life, that the kitchen is the center of our home. It's hard to believe I once thought I didn't need a cookbook.

---

**Tricia Stephens** was born and grew up in Dallas, Texas. She wrote comic books and poetry in high school. Since 2001 she has been writing stories in an SCN Internet Chapter writing circle to record her memories and as a way to learn about herself.

# Cinnamon Coffee Cake

## Ingredients

- 1½ cups flour
- ¾ cups sugar
- 2 teaspoons baking powder
- ½ teaspoon baking soda
- ½ teaspoon salt
- ½ teaspoon ground cinnamon
- ¼ cup oil
- ¾ cup milk
- 1 egg, lightly beaten

## Topping

- ⅓ cup brown sugar
- ¼ cup flour
- ½ teaspoon ground cinnamon
- 3 tablespoons crumbled butter

## Preparation

Preheat oven to 375°F.

Sift together the dry ingredients. Mix together the liquid ingredients and pour them into the dry ingredients. Beat with a whisk for ½ a minute. Pour batter into a greased 13x9-inch baking pan.

Combine the topping ingredients. Sprinkle the topping evenly over the batter. Bake for 30 minutes.

Makes one 13x9-inch cake.

## Tips and Notes

To make ahead, measure out the dry ingredients for several coffee cakes and the toppings, and seal them in airtight containers. Then all you have to do is add the liquid ingredients and a coffee cake is ready in 30 minutes.

**Georgia A. Hubley**

Sometimes it seems like yesterday, but it was a long time ago. Nevertheless, I can still hear my mom saying, "Here's the basket, please go to the henhouse and gather the eggs. I need an egg to make a chocolate cake." She didn't have to tell me twice; it meant there would be dessert after supper.

That's what we did on the farm back then, in the late 1940s. Desserts were made from scratch. There were no ready-made packages of cake mix. Mom's one-bowl chocolate cake was our family's favorite.

There was no electricity in our old farmhouse in Central Ohio. We'd never heard of an electric mixer. Mom beat the cake by hand, without a lump to be found. She'd quickly pour the creamy batter into a prepared square baking pan and place it into the oven of an old wood-burning kitchen stove. The cake baked while we were eating supper. Once it was baked, she'd let it cool slightly and then serve generous slices to us while it was still warm. There was no need for frosting as it was that tasty. Besides, it was wartime and sugar was being rationed. Frosting was something we learned to live without.

Mom never let hardships bother her. Her motto was, "We'll make do with what we have on hand." There were times when I took the basket to gather the eggs and there would be no eggs. Occasionally, an uninvited guest, a skunk, would sneak into the henhouse and steal the eggs before I got there.

Even when there were no eggs, it didn't hinder Mom from baking our favorite cake. She'd make her amazing Egg-less Chocolate Cake. We never could tell the difference. I can still recall that wonderful aroma of chocolate cake filling my nostrils as we eagerly waited for it to come from the oven. When I grew up, Mom passed down her Egg-less Chocolate Cake recipe to me.

*"Making It from Scratch" first appeared in the July 2003 issue of* Good Old Days *magazine.*

---

**Georgia A. Hubley** grew up in central Ohio. In 1996, she retired from 20 years in financial management and began writing her memoirs and submitting vignettes of her childhood for publication. Georgia has had six stories published in the *Chicken Soup for the Soul* series, as well as in many other national magazines and newspapers. Georgia lives with her husband in Henderson, Nevada. She has two grown sons.

# Egg-less Chocolate Cake

### Dry Ingredients

| | |
|---|---|
| 1¾ | cups sifted flour |
| 1 | cup granulated sugar |
| ¼ | cup cocoa |
| 1 | teaspoon baking soda |
| ½ | teaspoon salt |

### Wet Ingredients

| | |
|---|---|
| ⅓ | cup soft shortening |
| 1½ | teaspoon vanilla |
| 1 | tablespoon vinegar (white or cider) |
| 1 | cup cold water |

### Preparation

Preheat the oven to 350°F. Sift the dry ingredients together. Add the wet ingredients and beat well. Pour the batter into a greased 8-inch square pan that has been dusted with cocoa. Bake at 350°F. for 30–45 minutes.

Makes one 8-inch cake.

# Coconut Broiled Frosting

### Ingredients

| | |
|---|---|
| ¼ | cup melted butter or margarine |
| ½ | cup brown sugar, packed |
| ½ | teaspoon vanilla |
| ½ | cup shredded coconut |
| ¼ | cup chopped nuts |
| 2 | tablespoons evaporated or whole milk |

### Preparation

Combine all ingredients until smooth and spread on the warm cake still in the baking pan. Place under preheated broiler until frosting is bubbly, about 2 minutes. Watch closely, as frosting burns easily. Cool before cutting. Recipe is sufficient to top an 8-inch cake.

### Tips and Notes

This chocolate cake is delicious on its own. However, in later years my mother did occasionally add this broiled frosting to the cake.

---

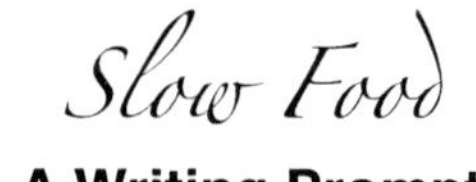


### A Writing Prompt

Back in the day, there was no such thing as "fast food." All food was "slow food" requiring our foremothers to spend many more hours in the kitchen than we do. Our families may have spent a good part of their lives growing, harvesting, and preserving food for later use, gathering wood for the kitchen stove, preparing the ingredients, and finally cooking the food that they ate every single day.

Did you ever help with gathering ingredients for family meals: picking vegetables in the garden, gathering eggs or fruit, or even running to the store for your mother? Choose one of these food memories and write a story about a "slow food" from your own childhood.

# Susan Ellen Ford's Annual Ribbon Cake

**Louise Saxon**

*I feel frantic. I can't find this recipe. It's been over one hundred years in the making, and careless me, I've let it slip away. Is it gone forever? Have I no memory? Perhaps I'll have to rely on that very thing, but is my memory slipping too?*

I remember my grandmother, Susan Ellen Ford, as a deeply religious soul with a strong will. She was born in 1856 and seemed very old by the time I came into the world. A serious woman, she wore her gray hair pulled back loosely into a bun. I do not recall ever seeing make-up on her face, and she usually wore clothes that seemed colorless or neutral in value. Still, she possessed a joyful and creative spark that showed itself in her remarkable crochet, hairpin lace, quilting, and tatting, and of course, in her very personal recipes, such as the Annual Ribbon Cake.

My grandmother met my grandfather in the foothills of the Arkansas Ozarks, near the little town of Viola. I do not remember hearing the exact circumstances, but they blended together like instant coffee and hot water and were wed in 1890. In the early years of marriage, they owned a 150-acre farm near Viola that boasted an apple orchard and at least a few peach trees. Life was reportedly tough, and they were often dirt poor, yet I am certain that Grandmother rose to many occasions by sheer willpower and creativity.

One Christmas, they had absolutely no money for gifts, but Grandmother did have plenty of flour and sugar in her larder and a number of peaches from their trees, which she had placed on the barn roof to dry. Her challenge was to put these ingredients together to make something very special for this most important occasion, the birthday of Christ. From that day forward, this delightful creation became an important part of the Ford family Christmas. When my grandparents took the bold step of moving to Texas, they hated to give up their apple orchard and peach trees, but the recipe came with them for generations to enjoy.

My mother, who died in 2005 at almost 104 years of age, made this cake faithfully throughout her lifetime. I took over when she could no longer make the effort. She would say, "Christmas just isn't Christmas without our annual cake."

*Now it's coming to me. Maybe there never was a written recipe after all. So many old recipes are passed along by word of mouth. In my mind's eye, I recall sitting at many holiday tables and visiting with relatives when the particulars of this cake were discussed. I close my eyes and focus hard to remember what happens first. Maybe I should check with my cousin, Martha James, for her take on the matter.*

*Ah, yes. I see my mother now, soaking the dried peaches in a pan to make them soft enough to reduce cooking time. During the last few minutes of cooking, it seems like she sprinkled in sugar and spices. At my suggestion, she daringly experimented one year by adding a dash of Cousin R. L.'s blackberry brandy for a bit of pizzazz. Grandmother, a teetotaler, might not have approved, but if you can get a little charge from a piece of cake, I say, go for it. This is how I like it. No sugar or spices are necessary for me.*

Grandmother's layers were always thin, but not so much so that the cake was ever soggy. How she did it,

Continues on page 122

# *Susan Ellen Ford's Annual Ribbon Cake*

### Ingredients for Cake Layers

| | |
|---|---|
| ½ | cup shortening |
| 2½ | cups sugar |
| 3 | eggs |
| 1 | cup buttermilk |
| 6 | cups flour, divided |
| 1 | teaspoon salt |
| ½ | teaspoon baking soda |
| 2 | teaspoons baking powder |

### Preparation

Cream the shortening and sugar, and add the eggs and buttermilk. Sift 2 cups of the flour together with salt, soda, and baking powder. Add the sifted dry ingredients to the creamed ingredients and mix.

Measure and sift 4 cups of flour into a large bowl. Pour the mixture into the sifted flour and mix to a stiff dough. Chill two hours or longer.

Preheat the oven to 350°F. Roll the dough out to 8x10-inch rectangles, each about ¼ inch thick. The dough should yield up to 10 layers. Bake each layer on a cookie sheet in a moderate oven (350°F.) for 8 minutes or more.

Once cool, put the layers together with the peach filling. Ice the top and sides with the same mixture.

### Ingredients for Peach Filling

| | |
|---|---|
| 2 | 12-ounce packages dried peaches |
| ⅛ | cup brandy, or to taste |

### Preparation

Soak the peaches in water to cover for two hours. When soft, stew them on top of the stove over low heat until a sauce forms for the filling. Cool, then blend in a blender and add the brandy, if desired. Refrigerate the filling until the layers are baked and ready to be stacked and iced.

Makes 1 large cake, about 8x10 inches, with about 10 layers.

### Tips and Notes

Watch layers carefully while cooking because thin layers burn easily.

Dried apricots can be substituted for some of the peaches, if desired.

A cooler filling is easier to spread.

---

**Louise Saxon** is an artist and a retired University of Texas Press fundraiser. Austin has always been home, but her salad days were spent in Houston, where she met her husband of almost thirty years. Widowed in 1990, she continued working at UT Press until 1999. These days, she hopes to spend as much time as possible painting and writing in the Northern Central New Mexico area, but sometimes this seems only like a dream.

Continued from page 120

I don't know. My cousin Martha does not roll out her layers. Instead, she presses and pats a heaping tablespoon of dough into a pie tin sprayed with Pam cooking spray. She always manages to make perfect thin layers as well, and so did our Aunt Ethel. My mother used the backs of cookie sheets, rolling the dough onto waxed paper cut to the size of the layers. That way there was no sticking and she could handle the cooked layers without breaking them. The paper should come off once the layers are out of the oven, but this method always looked like a lot of trouble. I cannot count on the thinness of mine. Always a klutz in the kitchen, my layers might depend on my ability to focus on the day I am rolling.

I love this cake and it always makes Christmas at my house complete. I'm so glad I reconstructed our treasured recipe and wrote it down so that others may be inspired to try it and include it in their own annual family traditions.

# Moose Milk

**Penny Leisch**

"Mom, what's a Tom and Jerry?" I asked, as I pulled a large punch set out of the closet. The front of the bowl said "Tom & Jerry" in bold red lettering.

"It's a drink," Mom answered.

"Do you and Dad drink those?"

"No. We use the bowl for Moose Milk."

I paused to consider her answer. Moose milk? I remembered seeing goat's milk in the grocery store but not moose milk.

"Mom, what's it taste like?" I asked, while I continued to rummage through the cupboard for the pan I needed to make a cake for the 4-H fair.

That punch set appeared every year during the holidays, but I never noticed what it contained. The adults drank their drinks, and I drank mine. But since I began cooking, my curiosity about everything cooking-related increased.

"Mom, how do you milk a moose?"

"How do you do what?" Mother sputtered as she tried to swallow her iced tea and laugh at the same time.

"How do you milk a moose?" I repeated.

"Oh, I see. Well, Moose Milk is your father's recipe for a drink. We don't really milk a moose. He made it years ago for a party and everyone loved it. So now we make it for our guests every year during the holidays. The liquor store in the shopping center even made up a recipe card to give their customers."

"It would be more fun if you really milked a moose."

"I suppose so, but I don't think the moose would cooperate. So we'll have to settle for this version. Now, what kind of cake are you making for your 4-H entry?"

# Penny's Quick Cinnamon Raisin Scones

### Scone Batter Ingredients

- 1 cup biscuit mix (use store-bought or double the biscuit mix recipe on page 127)
- 2 tablespoons sugar
- ½ teaspoon ground cinnamon
- ⅓ cup fat-free milk
- ½ cup dark raisins or chopped dates

### Topping

- 1 teaspoon ground cinnamon
- 1 teaspoon sugar

### Preparation

Pre-heat the oven to 425°F.

Combine the biscuit mix, 2 tablespoons of sugar, cinnamon, and milk to form a soft dough. Add the raisins or dates and stir only until they are blended throughout the dough. Drop the dough by spoonfuls onto an ungreased baking sheet.

In a small bowl, mix the cinnamon and sugar for the topping. Sprinkle lightly over the scones.

Bake the scones at 425°F. for 10 to 12 minutes, or until golden brown. Serve the scones warm.

Makes 4 servings.

# Moose Milk

**(Hot Rum Toddy)**

### Ingredients

- 1 tablespoon sweetened condensed milk (Eagle Brand)
- 1 ounce rum (or rum flavoring to taste)
- 4 ounces boiling water
- Nutmeg
- Whipped cream

### Preparation

In a coffee mug, mix the sweetened canned milk, rum, and boiling water. Garnish with a sprinkle of nutmeg and whipped cream, if desired.

Makes 1 serving. For larger quantities, increase ingredients equally.

---

**Penny Leisch** lives in Austin, Texas, with her husband and animals. She's a full-time freelance writer, entrepreneur, and photographer, who also has twenty years experience with animal rescue. Her writing appears in newspapers and magazines, anthologies, and online. She also taught Writing and Photography for Publication for the City of Tempe, Arizona. As an experienced pet rescuer, Penny writes and speaks about pet education and maintains a pet resource website too. Penny's websites are: www.pennyleisch.com and www.petsbypenny.com.

# *To Vicki,*

## *In Response to the Letter in Which She Teases, "In Your Honor, I Almost Doubled the Recipe"*

**Kathleen Rockeman**

Dear Girl,

It's not generosity or industry
That makes me overdo when guests come—
Rather, laziness and thrift.

It's the same time spent, I assure you, and every
bit the mess
To make a dozen sweet rolls as, say, a hundred.
The cost doesn't grow with the dough as it rises.
There are economies of scale.

With a dozen, you have merely breakfast.
With a hundred, you have a long sweet Sunday
Discovering just how many luscious buns can be
eaten slowly
Over pots and pots of coffee
With the neighbors who float in on the aroma.
You will suck sticky fingers and discuss subjects
That only surface when the kitchen smells
Of fresh-made bread and cinnamon
And good coffee and plenty.

With a hundred cinnamon rolls
You put by other lazy mornings
Double-wrapped in the basement freezer
Hidden behind the ground beef and bread flour,
Proof to the children sitting on the kitchen floor
together—
Laughing, lingering—
That no matter what they may have heard,
The world is a generous place.

There is more unhurried sweetness to be had
If they take the time to look.

---

**Kathleen Joslyn Rockeman** has always written poetry but didn't learn to bake until she was a new bride on a remote North Dakota cattle ranch. After mastering sweet rolls in branding-crew quantities, she took on more exotic cuisines as family moves took her overseas for twenty years. Her guiding principle for cooking and for living is: "Anything worth doing is worth overdoing."

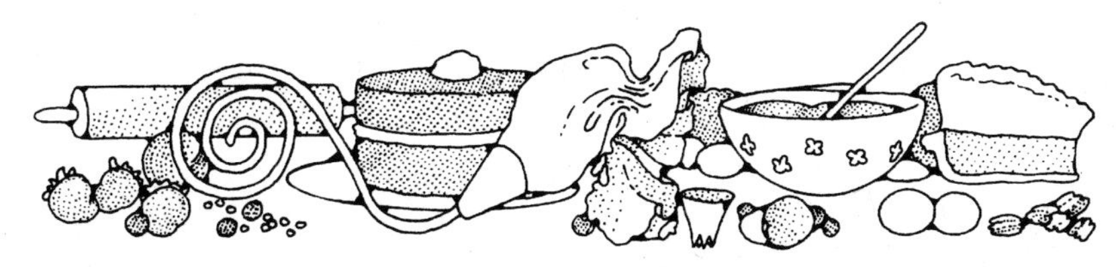

# *Sweet Pies and Desserts*

# *I'm Thankful for Mom's Pumpkin Pie*

**Rhonda Esakov**

For many years, Thanksgiving was a large production in our house, all choreographed by Mom. Family would come from miles around to attend our matriarch's delicious production of Thanksgiving dinner. When Mom died a few years ago, the families spread out and went their own ways and Dad retreated to a solitary condominium in the Ozarks. A few days before Thanksgiving in the year following Mom's passing, I received a cry for help from Dad. "Sis, I've been invited to Thanksgiving at your Aunt Beth's place and I need to bring a dessert. Can you help me? You know I can't cook very many things and everyone remembers how well your mother cooked. What can I do?"

Having inherited from Mom and Grandma the skill of cooking on the fly, I had the perfect solution to his dilemma—Mom's Easy Pumpkin Pie!

"Dad, I'm going to send you what you need to make a pumpkin pie and everyone will love it."

My next visit to the grocery store found me selecting all the ingredients I knew were not in Dad's skimpy larder, then I boxed it all up with a handwritten recipe to be shipped off to the Missouri Ozarks from my home in Texas. Then I crossed my fingers and waited until Thanksgiving Day.

On the afternoon of Thanksgiving Day, after I had cleared away the mess from our own family dinner that I had prepared for a large gathering of in-laws, children and adopted "near" cousins, I made the phone call to Missouri to my aunt's gathering of the clan. After words with half a dozen relatives, I finally got to speak with Dad. And his words were like bells signaling a new angel to my ears, and hopefully carried on to my mother's angel ears as well. "Sis, everyone thought the pie was wonderful and almost as good as your mom's. I just wish she had been here to enjoy it all without all the cooking she always had to do."

From your lips to her ears, Dad, I thought with a smile. And he fixes that same pie every year.

---

**Rhonda Esakov,** E.A., is a licensed tax preparer. When not working at her tax business, she enjoys visiting caves and teaching Hunter Education for Texas Parks and Wildlife along with outdoor courses for the Boy Scouts of America. Her writing includes articles for local publications, quarterly tax newsletters, and a memoir in progress on American children's experiences living in the Middle East.

# *Easy Pumpkin Pie*

### Ingredients

- ¾ cup sugar
- ½ cup biscuit mix
- 2 tablespoons butter
- 1 12-ounce can evaporated milk
- 2 teaspoons vanilla
- 2 eggs
- 1 16-ounce can pumpkin
- 1½ teaspoons ground cinnamon
- ½ teaspoon ground nutmeg
- ¼ teaspoon ground cloves
- ¼ teaspoon ground ginger

### Preparation

Preheat the oven to 350°F.

Grease a 9-inch or 10-inch pie pan. Place all ingredients into a blender and blend for 1 minute (or 2 minutes by mixer). Pour into the greased pie pan and bake 50–55 minutes. This makes a **big** pie! You do not need a separate pie crust for this pie; it forms its own light crust.

Serves 6–8.

### Tips and Notes

For variation, bake in an oblong 13x9-inch pan and spread with cream cheese frosting for delicious pumpkin bars.

If you prefer to use fresh pumpkin, select a 2–3-pound pumpkin and follow the directions on page 25 to prepare the pumpkin flesh.

**Homemade Biscuit Mix:** Combine ½ cup flour, ¾ teaspoon baking powder, ¼ teaspoon salt, and 2 teaspoons shortening in a food processor. Pulse on and off until well blended. Makes approximately ½ cup biscuit mix. Store in a cool dry place. (For 1 cup biscuit mix, double the ingredients.)

# *Making Apple Pie*

**Margaret Mallory**

Finding a good recipe for homemade apple pie is difficult these days. I have dozens of cookbooks but none with good apple pie recipes. Women once baked pies as a matter of course and thought nothing of it. Some women, but not many, still do.

Making a pie takes time and patience, requires advance planning, and cannot be hurried. On either a stay-at-home winter day, or a summer day, it is a series of meditative steps and an act of love.

In summer, on a porch with a rocking chair, and the apples in a bowl between your knees, the process begins.

Long chains of apple peel from the six apples are fragrant. The quartered and sliced apples go to the kitchen and are covered in sugar, flour, and cinnamon. Then there's the quick folding of flour, lard, and ice water for the crust using your fingers or a fork. The slender French rolling pin, just an ellipse of smooth wood, tapered at the ends, rolls out the dough on a circle of canvas, one for the bottom crust, one for the top.

Meanwhile the oven is heating and in goes the pie. After ten minutes the heat is reduced, and the house fills with a delicious aroma. Sometimes the oozing juices drip onto the oven floor and you wish you had remembered to put down a sheet of foil beneath the pie pan.

The pie is assembled in the evening, put to rest in the refrigerator over night, and baked in the cool of the following morning.

A basket is lined with a red and white checked cloth and the pie delivered to the children. The fluted edge is thick and irregular, not like the edge of the store-bought kind.

There is still the kitchen to clean, but the virtuous feeling remains. I have baked a pie.

Now that I have located the rolling pin, the canvas, the pastry blender, and the enormous box of lard, I must keep making pies. If I don't, my descendents will still be using all that lard, two-thirds of a cup at a time.

---

**Margaret Mallory** grew up in rural Minnesota and recently celebrated her ninetieth birthday in Austin, Texas, where she has lived since 1980. She's a mother, grandmother and great-grandmother, who has done a lot of interesting things over the years, including graphic arts and landscape gardening. During World War II Margaret was in San Francisco with the Red Cross. She raised four children who came eighteen months apart, so she always had an avid audience for her cooking and baking.

# Apple Pie

## Ingredients for Pie Crust Made with Lard for 1 Double-Crust Pie

| | |
|---|---|
| 1½ | cups flour |
| ½ | teaspoon salt |
| ⅔ | cup lard |
| 4 | tablespoons ice water |

## Filling Ingredients

| | |
|---|---|
| 6 | apples, peeled, cored and cut into eights |
| ⅔–¾ | cup sugar (depending on tartness of apples) |
| 1 | tablespoon flour |
| ¼ | teaspoon ground cinnamon |
| | Butter |
| | Lemon juice |

## Preparation

Preheat the oven to 450°F.

Mix the dry ingredients for the crust. Rub in lard. Add ice water and blend lightly to make a smooth dough. Roll out on lightly floured waxed paper or canvas and line a 9-inch pie pan.

Mix the apple slices, sugar, flour, and cinnamon. Fill the dough-lined pie pan with apples, dot with butter, and sprinkle one tablespoon lemon juice on top.

Slit the upper crust for steam vents. Lay it over the pie and seal the crusts. Trim the dough to ½ inch from the edge; turn under the dough and flute.

Bake at 450°F. for 10 minutes, reduce heat to 375°F., and bake about 35 minutes longer.

Makes 1 pie.

# Aunt Edith's Lemon Meringue Pie

**Linda Joy Myers**

The tastes and memories of childhood create a longing in our hearts for times we'll never see again, for people whose faces glance at us in frayed sepia tones between the pages of a scrapbook. I yearn for summer afternoons in Iowa with my great-aunts and great-grandmother Blanche. Long, light days with ripe, red tomatoes, watermelon, and hordes of relatives at the kitchen table.

Every summer my grandmother, my guardian since my mother left when I was five, would drive the pink Nash Rambler to the farm near Muscatine, Iowa, a mile from the great Mississippi river. On hot summer nights Blanche and I would lie on the featherbed where she told me stories. Born three years before Custer's Last Stand, she married Lewis on New Year's Day—two months later he died of pneumonia. Blanche was pregnant with my grandmother. She married again and had six more children, including my Aunt Edith. She was a little different from the rest of my generously endowed great-aunts—thin, soft-spoken with blue eyes like me. All of Blanche's girls knew how to cook great meals, except my grandmother. I learned to cook when I was ten from Aunt Edith.

Edith's kitchen was heaven. It gleamed and sparkled, this white, modern, fifties kitchen complete with electric stove, a mixer, and a utility room with its washer and dryer. Blanche spit every time she saw that washer and dryer sitting there so primly—not so long ago, she'd had to wash her clothes in a pot boiling in the front yard.

## Making the Pie

Aunt Edith measures a cup of flour and a third cup of Crisco into a bowl, mixes it into crumbly pieces, and pours in enough cold water for it gather itself into a ball. The ball goes onto the floured table where we roll it in a circle with the rolling pin. The ballet of this pie is accompanied by the sound of ticking clocks, ticking away the time of my childhood, the time we are using now to make our pie, until one day time will stop as everyone here—my grandmother, Blanche, and Edith, even my mother in far away Chicago—will all leave to enter that other world. I wonder if there is lemon meringue pie up there—wherever that is.

But today, it seems we will all live forever. Edith shapes a round, perfect world of crust and slides it into the metal pie pan. I love crimping the soft dough between my fingers and thumb. Her crimps are high and proud. Some things in this world can be controlled, brought into alignment with the proper technique.

Next, there's the lemon pudding and meringue. Edith teaches me how to break eggs so not a speck of yolk escapes. I whip the egg whites into froth. We pour the thick, yellow pudding into the crust, using a spatula to

*Continues on page 132*

---

**Linda Joy Myers** is the author of *Becoming Whole: Writing Your Healing Story*. Her memoir *Don't Call Me Mother* won the 2006 Gold Medal Award through the Bay Area Independent Publishing Association. Linda Joy learned how to cook from her Iowa aunts, and still loves to fix "real food" for family, friends, and her three grandchildren. Linda teaches memoir workshops nationally and in the San Francisco Bay Area. She is working on her first novel, which is set during World War II.

# Aunt Edith's Lemon Meringue Pie

### Ingredients for Pie Crust Made with Shortening/Butter for 1 Single-Crust Pie

- ½ cup vegetable shortening and butter combination
- 1 generous cup flour
- Pinch of salt
- ¼ cup cold water, approx.

### Preparation

Preheat the oven to 425°F.

Mix the flour and salt in a large bowl. Add the shortening and mix with your fingertips. Add water gradually until the mixture starts to gather into a ball. Too much water makes the crust too sticky; too little makes it dry. Gather the mixture into a ball and place it on a floured board. With a floured rolling pin, roll out all the edges into a round world of dough. Place the dough in a 9-inch pie pan. Poke holes in bottom to help the crust lie down in the pan.

Bake pie crust at 425°F. for 10 minutes, then cool.

### Tips and Notes

Use a non-hydrogenated stick butter replacement such as Earth Balance with butter for a healthy, modern update for the crust instead of Crisco or butter alone.

Aunt Edith always made her lemon meringue pie using Jell-o pie filling. To make the lemon pie filling from scratch, use the ingredients listed at right. Whisk the first 6 ingredients together over medium heat until boiling. Remove from heat and add butter. Spoon into pie shell, top with meringue, and bake.

### Ingredients for Easy Pie Filling

- 1 2.9-ounce package Jell-o "Cook & Serve" lemon pudding and pie mix
- ½ cup sugar
- 2¼ cups water, divided
- 2 egg yolks
- 3 egg whites
- 1 tablespoon sugar

### Preparation

Stir the lemon pie mix, ½ cup of sugar, ¼ cup of water, and 2 egg yolks in a medium saucepan. Stir in 2 cups of water. Stirring constantly with a whisk, cook on medium heat until mixture comes to a full boil. Spoon the pudding mix into the baked and cooled pie shell.

Whip 3 egg whites with 1 tablespoon of sugar into a frothy meringue. Pile on top of the pudding in the pie shell. Bake at 350°F. for 15–20 minutes or until the meringue is golden.

Cool the pie before cutting, but it is a great treat to eat it warm with fresh-made coffee.

Makes 1 pie.

### Ingredients for "From-Scratch" Pie Filling

- 1 cup water
- ⅔ cup sugar
- ⅓ cup fresh lemon juice
- 4 egg yolks
- 3½ tablespoons cornstarch
- 1½ tablespoons grated lemon peel
- 1½ tablespoons butter

*Continued from page 130*

mound the meringue in little peaks. After ten minutes, we take the pie out of the oven and proudly place it in the middle of the table. The meringue has golden peaks, and everyone gathers around to admire our handiwork.

Edith and I make lemon meringue pie for the next forty years. Every year of my childhood and into my adulthood I come to this house by the Mississippi River to get a taste of my roots, despite the mother who disfavors me and the silence of the dead around us.

Even on that last August day, Edith and I had planned to make pie when we got the call that my mother had died. We sat at the kitchen table and cried for her and for all the ones we'd lost, the clocks still ticking. After that she wiped her eyes and got out the glass bowl, the flour tin, the Crisco. She clutched her side, already on her own downward slide toward that other world, but together, step by step, we made lemon meringue pie that hot August day, sweat dripping down our faces.

When it was done and the meringue was golden, we sliced it and placed it onto plates. We cut an extra piece for Gram, for Blanche, and for my mother. There could have been a table full of invisible guests, but we stopped there. She perked the coffee as we always had, and as if we knew this was the last time, she lifted her fork to me. "A toast," she grinned, and scooped the pie into her mouth. Our pie was still warm, still fresh from our efforts. All our years together tasted sweet in my mouth. Edith and I savored our lemon meringue pie as if it was the last pie we would ever make. And it was.

## Pie Crust Made with Butter for 1 Single-Crust Pie

### Ingredients

- 1¼ cups all purpose flour or pastry flour
- ½ tablespoon sugar
- ½ teaspoon salt
- ½ cup (1 stick) chilled unsalted butter, cut into ½-inch cubes
- 3 tablespoons (or more) ice water

### Preparation

Blend the flour, sugar, and salt in a food processor. Add the butter and cut in, using on/off turns, until a coarse meal forms. Add 3 tablespoons water. Using on/off turns, blend just until moist clumps form, adding more water by ½ tablespoonfuls if the dough is dry. Remove the dough from the food processor. Form the dough into a ball and flatten it into a disk. Wrap in plastic or waxed paper; refrigerate for 1 hour.

Makes one 9-inch single crust.

### Tips and Notes

To make the dough by hand, gently rub the butter into the dry ingredients. When the mixture has the consistency of cornmeal, add water and form into a ball of dough.

For 1 double-crust pie or 2 single-crust pies, double the ingredients. Divide the dough in half, and form 2 disks before refrigerating.

For 2 double-crust pies, multiply the ingredients by 4.

This pastry can be made 2 days ahead. Keep chilled. Soften slightly at room temperature before rolling.

# Supermarket Showdown

**Annabelle Bailey**

Cereal. High fiber? Low calorie? A combination
of both?
A food staple or something for the stable?
Do I have time to read the label?
Fruits and vegetables—a minefield
Do I dare to eat a carb? Good carb. Bad carb.
White potato, stand back!
Is that a domestic orange? Might I hope—
organic?
Be very afraid—high-glycemic corn and carrots
Bean sprouts low-cal but bacteria friendly
Rinse your veggies well
But only time will tell.
I think I have the system down!
Eggs all natural—free range.
No preservatives, feel well!
On no, what's that smell? Cheese expired.
Nearing the end, checkout, tabloid skirmish
Wonder diet on page 16?
Recipe for chocolate layer cake page 17?
Weight Watcher point system?
Hire someone to point out the bad foods?
Almost over—I can see the parking lot.
Shopper card? Paper or plastic?
No more questions, please!

# Dad's Nut Pies

## Ingredients

| | |
|---|---|
| | Pie crust (use the double recipe on page 132 or two 9-inch, store-bought pie crusts) |
| 2 | cups brown sugar |
| ½ | cup butter |
| 2 | eggs |
| ½ | cup milk |
| 1 | cup chopped walnuts |
| 1 | cup sweetened flaked coconut |
| 2 | cups chopped raisins |

## Preparation

Preheat the oven to 350°F.

Make (or buy) the pie crust. If you're making your own pie crust, roll the pastry out to about ¼ inch thick.

Cut the pastry into 3-inch rounds using a cookie cutter or the rim of a glass. Fit the rounds into aluminum cupcake liners. Mix all other ingredients in a large bowl. Fill the miniature pie shells with the mixture. Bake at 350°F. until the crust is golden, about 25 minutes.

Makes 24 small pies.

---

**Annabelle Bailey** lives in Connecticut with her husband. She is a former English and Spanish teacher with a degree in gerontology. Retired now, Annabelle spends much of her time enjoying two of her favorite hobbies, writing and painting.

# *Aunt Kate's Coconut Chess Pie*

**Bonnie Watkins**

"I got that pie recipe from Lil Shullock when she was in her fifties, and she got it from Ruth Gibson when she was in her eighties, and Ruth said she got it from her mama. When people ask me, I tell them it's over 200 years old, since I'm getting on up in years too," Aunt Kate says, adding, "It's not made from anything special, just things you'd always have on hand and you can fix it up quick if company comes unexpected."

Although she may be "getting on up in years," Aunt Kate has more flowers and more energy in her eighties than many folks much younger. She has needed it. One scorching summer day in 1936, her young husband came in from the fields at noon to eat. He felt something annoying behind his knee. Investigating, Victor found a tick that he pulled out and went right back to the fields.

Several days later, he said to Kate, "The back of my knee's sore. I must have left that tick head in. Can you get it?"

"I got it. Hold still," Kate said and jerked with her tweezers. Back Victor went to work.

A few more days passed, and he began to notice that the flesh was rotting around the tick bite. A nickel-sized hole followed and then a lump the size of a turkey egg on his leg. The doctor lanced it, but the poison had already traveled into his system. In the hospital, he was unconscious for thirteen days and had seven spinal taps, but Victor was paralyzed from his waist down.

Most everyone in the small German and Czech community of Moulton, Texas, farmed. Other jobs were already getting scarce, but then when the war broke out, they were virtually impossible to find. Victor and Kate took over a grocery store—a tiny, one car Model T garage with a wooden floor converted into a store—thinking that folks will always have to eat.

Mornings, Kate sat Victor in the store with a bell that he rang when customers came. She heard it in the house next door and came out to pump the rationed gas: five gallons for seventy-seven cents. Brooms cost thirty-five cents and cigarettes seventeen cents a pack. Raisins, prunes, dried apples and peaches came in twenty-five-pound wooden boxes, and Kate sacked pound bags for customers. Fresh apples and oranges also came in wooden boxes but only at Christmas. Lard came in five-gallon cans. People brought their containers, and Kate sold them the amount they wanted.

"God is good, and people are good too," Kate recalls. "On Sundays, friends, kinfolks, neighbors and town people came to our little store and almost bought us out. They spent the evening sitting on tree roots; some brought stools or sat on two old benches we had under a big live oak tree. The children had an old gentle horse they rode. Once when a Volkswagen drove by, one lady said, 'Well, you can see anything out here, even a Hitler car.' On Monday morning I drove back into town to stock up again for the store."

A tiny tick drove Kate from a homemaker and mother who reveled in propagating a larger and fuller hydrangea to a businesswoman who learned ledger columns, pumped gas, and toted heavy boxes. For seventeen loving years she cared for her paralyzed husband until he died too young at thirty-nine.

Kate's fetching smile was framed by jet black, curly hair and tender, deep brown eyes. She laughed freely and provided a willing audience for all the corny country jokes that came through the slamming screen door of her grocery store.

For years my dad's brother Milton enjoyed Kate's good cheer and pretty face and figure. With his repertoire of jokes getting longer and longer, he often visited Fisbeck's Grocery and tried to get an extra look from Kate, along with all the other men in town. After thirteen years, he won her over and Kate Fisbeck became Kate Higgins.

Now when our family sits over a piece of warm coconut chess pie, Uncle Milton might say, "Have you heard the one about the priest and the Baptist minister?"

"Oh, Milton," Kate will demur, "don't tell that one. It's too bad." But underneath, a smile plays on her lips, and she knows that Milton will tell it with every detail to make it funnier.

That's when we settle in for another piece of Aunt Kate's pie.

# Aunt Kate's Coconut Chess Pie

### Ingredients

- 2 unbaked pie shells (see pie crust recipe on page 132)
- 2 cups sweetened, shredded coconut
- 1 cup milk (whole)
- 2 cups sugar
- 1 stick margarine, melted
- 4 eggs
- 1 teaspoon vanilla
- 1 cup pecans, chopped fine

### Preparation

Preheat the oven to 350°F.

Prepare the pie shells. Mix the ingredients a little. Do not whip. Pour the batter into the 2 unbaked pie shells. Bake at 350°F. for 30 minutes until golden brown.

Makes 2 pies.

---

**Bonnie Watkins** has been a teacher all her life, teaching ages two to ninety-two. Currently, she teaches American Literature, Communication Applications, and Creative Writing at Hyde Park Baptist High School in Austin, Texas. For several years she wrote a monthly column, "Making Money at Home," for *Welcome Home* magazine. She has published parenting and teaching articles, as well as poems and devotionals. Currently, Bonnie belongs to the Wordweavers Story Circle Network writing circle.

# *Not as Easy as Rhubarb Pie*

**Erin Declan Philbin**

In the summer of my twelfth year, I learn to bake pies. Mom coaches me through making the crust, adding an occasional comment about women who don't make their own. She teaches me to light the pilot on our huge old gas stove, using a piece of straw plucked from our broom. I'm always careful to keep my distance. Mom shares stories of friends who leaned too close and burned off their eyebrows, leaving them looking surprised all the time until they grew back. After a few lessons, I'm on my own. When I'm in the kitchen, I'm queen of my kingdom. I have the superiority that only a twelve year old can muster.

I love baking pies—the feel of the dough coming together under my fingers, the rhythm of rolling and flipping the crust until it is a consistent thinness. My favorite pie is rhubarb. They aren't popular with my friends, but I love the rhubarb's unexpected tartness. While I bake, I chomp on stalks of it as if it were celery.

I am content in my "pie queen" place until one night when my mother calls me into the kitchen. She and my dad have just said goodbye to friends after an evening of coffee, conversation, and pie. "My friends have never learned to bake pie, and you know what that means," Mom says. I wait for the punch line. "It means they have never *had* to bake a pie," Mom says looking me straight in the eye.

"What the heck does that mean?" I ask.

"It means that while you and I were baking pies, they were doing something else, like reading," Mom replies. This rocks my whole world. I love baking pies, but I love reading more. Over the next several years, I spend less and less time in the kitchen.

After grad school, I marry Chris, a man who does not have a sweet tooth. He also prefers to do all the cooking. Hey, I'm a smart girl; I let him!

I develop a new ritual of taking myself out for dessert. I go to lovely bakeries, coffee houses, and tea shops and order delicious, decadent desserts. When our sons are born, nine and thirteen years later, I'm thrilled to make it a tradition. We enjoy our time together, sharing stories, cakes, biscotti, and tiramisu.

All is well until a snowy Saturday right before Christmas. The boys are eight and four, and I don't feel right about taking them out on the roads. In a flash of inspiration, I pull out a roll of Rudolph "slice and bake" cookies that Chris has bought. The cookies baking will warm the house and make it smell great.

With one smooth gesture, I pop the tube open and nearly drop the roll on the floor. The kids run in to check on me. I pick up a knife to make the first slice. "Stop!" Brendan yells. "You're not allowed to touch knives!"

"Sure I am," I assure him. I slice the first cookie. Rudolph's face squishes a bit. "It makes him look like he's

---

**Erin Declan Philbin** was born into a loving family, the fourth of five girls. She is a speech-language pathologist in a rehabilitation hospital in Pittsburgh. She is married to Christopher Boyle, who gives her the encouragement and time to write. Her sons, Brendan (twelve) and Owen (eight), are the inspiration for many of her stories. She joined Story Circle in 1997 to create some balance in her life and to share the small stories that make her life.

concentrating on keeping his nose lit," I joke. By the third slice, Rudolph looks cross-eyed. By the fifth, he looks like he got his head slammed in the door of Santa's sleigh. I start making thicker slices.

It's time to pop the cookies in the oven. "Wait!" yells a horrified Brendan. "Only Daddy is allowed to turn on the stove!" I have to phone my husband to confirm that I have permission to light the oven. I open its door but can't find where to light the pilot. After several minutes, I have no choice but to call my husband again, discovering that pilot lights on stoves no longer need to be lit.

"What temperature are you supposed to bake the cookies," Chris asks, deciding to talk me through the process. I retrieve the wrapper from the garbage and read off the number.

"Wait a minute! There are no numbers on the oven dial!" I wail.

"I was so excited when we got the new oven, I accidentally scrubbed them off," Chris responds. "Just turn the dial about 168 degrees southwest."

"Wait while I go find a compass and a protractor," I snarl.

Chris suggests that I set the dial so it looks like ten minutes to four. I set the timer—yes, I know how—and we wait. Before long, the house is filled with the lovely smell of scorched cookies. The thinner ones are burning while the thicker ones are raw. I rescue two only slightly charred Rudolphs and present one to each kid.

I take a look outside where the snow continues to fall steadily. "Hey kids!" I say. "Who wants to go out for some cheesecake?"

# Not as Easy as Rhubarb Pie

### Ingredients for Pie Crust Made with Crisco for 2 Double-Crust Pies

- 3 cups flour
- ½ teaspoon salt
- ½ teaspoon baking powder
- 1 cup Crisco
- 4 tablespoons sugar
- ¼ cup milk

### Filling Ingredients

- 1½ cups rhubarb, cut into 1-inch pieces
- 1 cup sugar
- 1 cup raisins
- 1 egg
- ½ teaspoon salt
- 1 tablespoon flour
- ½ teaspoon lemon juice

### Preparation

Preheat the oven to 375°F. Mix the dry ingredients together. Add Crisco and blend. Slowly add the milk. You may not need all of it. Form a ball of dough, handling it as little as possible. Cut the dough into 4 pieces. These are the tops and bottoms for 2 pies. Roll out 4 circles of dough and use the 2 larger ones to line the bottom of 2 pie pans.

Mix all the filling ingredients together and add to the pie crust. Cover with the other circles of dough. Wrap aluminum foil around the edges of the pie crust so it won't burn. Bake at 375°F. for around 40 minutes. Remove the foil from around the crust of the pie and continue baking 15–20 minutes longer until the crust is golden brown. Makes 2 pies.

# *Snow Cream*

**Pat Turner**

I hear it again! I hear the childlike delight in my mother's voice for making snow cream.

Snow does not occur often in Memphis, Tennessee, where I was raised. Even when it does snow, it may not be very deep. But snow days are magical. I watch anxiously and hope there will be enough of an accumulation by the time Mother gets home from work. If there is enough, we will make snow cream.

My sister, little brother, and I are giddy with anticipation, watching from the back door as Mother scoops fresh snow into the big soup pot and slips and slides with it as she heads back into the house. I smell the sugar and vanilla that we hurriedly mix into the snow creating a soft slushy mixture. I hear the giggles and the ping of spoons in bowls and the scrape of the big spoon against the metal pot. We mix and eat it quickly, because it melts really fast. We know we can also freeze some for later.

I taste the sweetness and feel the cold in my throat—surely no ice cream could ever be this cold. I feel the warmth of our small kitchen glowing with love. Treats are few. Money is scarce and Mother works hard to support us. But no store-bought treat could ever equal snow cream.

Years later I call Mother to ask how to make snow cream for my son. Although there was never a written recipe, she shares the list of ingredients and approximate measurements. Today I hardly ever experience snow, but hearing the delight in Mother's voice takes me back to those magical days when we would make snow cream.

---

**Pat Turner** is a recently retired grandmother, who anticipates spending more time on creative pursuits, including writing. She and her husband retired after twenty-five years of retail store ownership. She has facilitated the Memory Keepers Story Circle in Tyler, Texas, for five years after discovering Story Circle Network in a writing magazine. Because she believes strongly in the importance of preserving our stories, she is delighted to be a part of Story Circle Network.

# Mamaw Jones' Snow Cream

### Ingredients

| | |
|---|---|
| 1 | big pot of snow (or finely shaved ice) |
| 1 | egg, beaten |
| ⅓ | cup sugar |
| 1 | teaspoon vanilla |
| | Cold milk |

### Preparation

Mix the egg, sugar, and vanilla. Blend all ingredients into the snow, together with enough milk to create a soft creamy texture. Enjoy some now (it melts quickly). Freeze some for later.

### Tips and Notes

Back then, Mother used eggs fresh from the neighborhood grocery store or the local farm. That was before factory farming and the fear of Salmonella in raw eggs. Pasteurized eggs were unheard of. Nowadays pasteurized egg products are recommended over raw egg.

---

## The Flavors of the Season

### A Writing Prompt

When we were young, each season had its own special foods, foods that we ate only at that time of the year because the ingredients weren't available at other times. Like snow cream in winter or pumpkin pie in the fall. Perhaps your family had its own special seasonal foods, foods whose ingredients were plentiful in your garden or your region for a short time each year. Think back to the special seasonal foods of your childhood. Remember how the temperature of the air, the special smell of the season, would conjure up thoughts of that particular food.

Make a list of the sights, smells, tastes, and textures of one or more of your own special seasonal foods from childhood and of the season that went with it. Now write a story about one of these seasonal foods.

# *Organoleptically Speaking*

**Lavon Urbonas**

Fat and sweet and slightly tart—that's how I like my comfort foods.

Fat is satisfying, soothing, sensual. It lolls on the tongue and palate, bathing the taste buds with the flavors dissolved in it, thus extending the pleasure beyond the first moment. By itself, however, it can overwhelm with heaviness.

Sweet alone is empty. That primitive urge to obtain quick energy in the form of sugar leads to an unquenched craving. The sense of it dissipates too soon. The initial delight teases but does not stay.

Tart has pucker power on its own, but in judicious amounts it adds piquant and pungent punctuation marks that make the taste buds stand up and say, "Goody!"

The combination of any two of these—but preferably all three—produces a gustatory experience that is greater than the sum of its parts: not cloying, but rich and sometimes downright decadent.

The epitome of an organoleptic experience is my consummate comfort food, cheesecake. It touches my psyche and my soul, as well as my soma. The creaminess evokes that first food, mother's milk, and conjures up images of cows and dairy products that are synonymous with my Swiss roots. The butterfat that lingers in my mouth long after I've swallowed the last bite substitutes for a soothing massage. The graham cracker crust adds a sweet crunchy contrast to the smoothness, taking me back to my childhood when graham crackers were a treat, especially when slathered with real butter whenever we could afford it. The essence of vanilla stirs memories of aromas wafting from kitchens past. The tang of the sour cream tempers the sweetness and sharpens my senses so that each individual flavor stands out in the perfect melding of ingredients.

Look at it sitting there, beckoning. That cheesecake! Its circularity connotes completeness and is elegant in its simplicity. It is dense and packed full of promises—promises to banish the blues, assuage anger, fell fears—promises it never fails to deliver, along with an abundance of divinely, devilishly delicious calories. Cheesecake is Comfort with a capital C.

---

**Lavon Urbonas** used to write about food as a Registered Dietitian, but she's finding it a lot more fun now that she's retired and creative writing has become her hobby. Everyday events inspire short stories, poems, and memoirs. She is proud that several of her stories, not all of them food related, have appeared in the *Story Circle Journal*.

# *Beth's Cheesecake*

### Ingredients

#### Graham Cracker Crust

- ¼ cup butter, melted
- 1½ cups graham cracker crumbs
- 1 tablespoon sugar
- ¼ teaspoon ground cinnamon

#### Filling

- 4 large eggs
- 35 ounces cream cheese (four 8-ounce packages plus one 3-ounce package)
- 1 tablespoon vanilla
- 1 pint sour cream
- ½ cup sugar
- ½ cup buttermilk
- ¼ cup butter, melted

### Preparation

Preheat the oven to 300°F.

Melt ½ cup of butter. Set aside ¼ cup of the melted butter for the pie filling. Mix together the graham cracker crumbs, the sugar, and the cinnamon. Dribble in ¼ cup melted butter and mix. Press into bottom of a 10-inch spring-form pan.

In a large bowl, use an electric mixer to beat the eggs until light and fluffy. Break in the cream cheese bit by bit. When the mixture is creamy, add vanilla, sour cream, and ½ cup sugar, and continue mixing. Add enough buttermilk to make the batter the consistency of pancake batter. Add the ¼ cup melted butter that you set aside; mix. Pour into the crust.

Bake for 45 minutes at 300°F. Remove the cheesecake from the oven and immediately place it in refrigerator. When it is cool, cover the cheesecake with plastic wrap and let it chill a minimum of 8 hours.

Makes 10–12 servings.

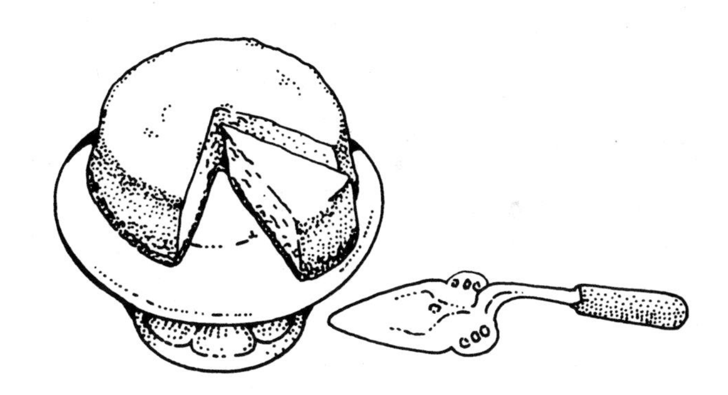

# *Grandma Thompson's Kitchen*

**Beth van Duzer**

One of my favorite pictures from my childhood is of me and my three siblings seated around my Grandma and Grandpa Thompson's kitchen table eating a hearty breakfast of chocolate pop-tarts on 1970s olive green plates. Growing up, we only saw our maternal grandparents one week out of the year. Every summer our vacation would take us from Northern New Jersey to Central Tennessee to visit my mother's relatives. One of the things I remember most about these vacations is my Grandmother's cooking and her kitchen. Even though the kitchen was small, it never felt too crowded or like the four of us were underfoot. We were always welcome. Perhaps it was because my mother felt more at ease with her family than with my father's family that us kids also felt more at ease to act as we normally would around home. Or, perhaps it was because my grandparents only saw us once a year that they were more willing to put up with four noisy, not always perfectly behaved children better than my other relatives we saw more often. Whatever the case, I just know that food made in my Grandma Thompson's kitchen tasted great.

Grandma Thompson cooked foods we normally did not get at home or, even if my mother made them at home, Grandma Thompson's just tasted better. On one occasion my grandmother fried up quail for everyone. The adults all stood around the kitchen table while us kids sat in chairs just reaching for food off the platters and eating without a care for a plate—napkins did just fine. Everyone was chatting animatedly as they ate their quail and drank their Coca-Cola. I remember us kids were tickled by the kid-sized birds and amazed that they tasted like chicken.

The fondest memory I have of my Grandma's kitchen is her peach cobbler. The recipe was easy. It never took her long to assemble the dish. As the cobbler cooked you could smell the peach juice melding with the cake and in your head you knew that the gooey part where the cake and juice met was the tastiest and that was the piece you wanted. As soon as the cobbler was out of the oven, everyone who was in the house gathered around the stove, with spoon in hand, ready to eat the hot dessert right out of the pan. When we were little we were not allowed to partake in this tradition, but as we grew older we were permitted to eat out of the pan with the adults. I think that the cobbler eaten hot out of the pan was the best cobbler I ever ate in my life! Maybe that was part of the reason the food tasted so good. We got to do things we normally were not allowed to do.

My grandmother died in the summer of 1993. My mother has passed a few of Grandma Thompson's recipes down to me, including the one for peach cobbler. I have tried making it but it just doesn't taste the same as hers. I do plan on making the dessert for my daughters and telling them about their great-grandmother—as soon as I can perfect the recipe. Maybe all I need to do is let my kids run around making noise while I assemble the dish, just like my grandma used to do when making it for us.

# Grandma Thompson's Peach Cobbler

### Ingredients

1 29-ounce can peaches with juice
1 cup self-rising flour
1 cup sugar
1 cup milk
1 stick butter

### Preparation

Preheat the oven to 375°F.

Mix the flour and sugar together. Add the milk to the dry ingredients and mix well to make a batter.

Melt 1 stick of butter in an 8x8-inch or 9x9-inch baking pan. Pour the batter into the pan with melted butter. **Do not stir.** Pour the peaches and juice over the mixture in the pan. **Do not stir.**

Bake at 375°F. for 45–60 minutes.

Serves 4–6.

---

**Beth van Duzer** is a stay-at-home mom in Georgetown, Massachusetts. She enjoys making mud pies as well as real pies with her daughters. In her free time she reads, writes and is copresident of her local mother's club, The Mother Connection. She submits stories of her family's mishaps to SCN as well as *Motherwords*, a regional magazine for Northeast Massachusetts and Southern New Hampshire.

# *Mama's Peachy Kitchen*

**Bonnie Watkins**

Surely no kitchen will ever hold more memories than the one where we received the most meals: our own mama's.

Unlike my own narrow galley kitchen, Mama's kitchen was huge with spacious ceilings and a window where dishwashing wasn't much of a chore because we looked out on lush bushes and red day lilies that she had planted. At first, it had wooden "drainboards" as we called countertops in the '50s. Later, it was re-modeled with ceramic tile and even a dishwasher. Not only can I close my eyes and see Mama working at that sink, but I can also see Daddy right before bed with his handful of saltines and his glass of milk.

Even more memories surround the breakfast room, that tiny nook where we took so many meals together. Of course, with school lunches being served on a light green plastic tray with a rectangular meat section, two square vegetable sections, a round dessert section, and a spot for the small red box of milk, and all for thirty-five cents, I mostly remember breakfast and supper at home. Daddy had been up since four a.m. milking the cows when he took a break, left his rubber boots on the back porch, and came in to the hearty fare he needed, almost always bacon, eggs fried in the grease (no thoughts of cholesterol then), orange juice and coffee, and toast from the electric toaster that sat on the table to pop up golden thin slices of Pepperidge Farm bread (Mama always found the best brands) to slather with butter and jam.

Supper (country folks didn't call the evening meal "dinner") was usually our own butchered beef from a huge chest-type freezer. We regularly enjoyed rump and rib roasts, pot roasts, meat loaf, and steak. Even the liver was good fried with plenty of onions. Mama boiled the tongue and heart and sliced them thin for delicious sandwiches. Along with the generous portions of meat, we usually had two healthy vegetables and/or a fruit salad.

One of my fondest memories is what I called "love from the oven in an aluminum pie tin." By high school and the time that I could drive, I was always involved in drama rehearsals after school and usually got home late. Before the days of microwaves, Mama would save my supper in that pie tin covered with foil. It was always so delicious after a long day at school.

Of the many possibilities of Mama's recipes, I think that two of my favorites involve peaches. The first is my favorite type of recipe of all: so simple, with ingredients always in your pantry and one of those that you have in your head and can just make in a minute without consulting a recipe. The second takes a little more work but is well worth it. I serve it often in the summer if we can find good peaches, and it's wonderful for company served with ice cream, whipped cream, or poured half and half.

*Read Bonnie Watkins' biography on page 135.*

## Broiled Peaches

### Ingredients

1 8-ounce can peach halves
Brown sugar
Ground cinnamon

### Preparation

Open the can of peaches. Drain and discard the juice. Spread the peaches in a pie plate. Sprinkle with brown sugar and cinnamon. Place under the broiler until the sugar has melted.

Serves 4–6.

### Tips and Notes

This is one of those "pantry dishes" that one always has on hand with the canned peaches. It wouldn't be the same with fresh ones because of the firm texture and added sugar of the canned ones.

Broiled peaches are delicious as a dessert or served on the side with pork.

## Peach Dumplings

### Ingredients

3 cups sliced fresh peaches
2 cups water
1 cup sugar
2 tablespoons lemon juice
1 cup pancake mix
¼ cup brown sugar
¼ teaspoon nutmeg
½ cup milk (at least 2%)
2 tablespoons vegetable oil

### Preparation

Combine the peaches, water, sugar, and lemon juice in a 3-quart pan. Bring to a boil. Combine the remaining ingredients, stirring lightly. Drop the batter from a tablespoon onto the hot peach mixture. Reduce heat; cover tightly. Cook for 15 minutes without lifting the cover. Serve warm.

Serves 6–8.

# *Food Memories*

**Janet Caplan**

I still love to cook and I especially still love to bake, admittedly not the way I did when I was younger and first married. Before the arrival of children, when I seemed to have more time for everything, I loved to experiment with recipes for Saturday evening dinners with friends and family. Times have changed and so has my desire to spend limitless hours in the kitchen, although, given the right frame of mind on a cool Sunday afternoon, who knows what smells might emanate from my oven or cook top. The memories of those early days of my marriage are certainly vivid for many reasons, but food definitely plays a major role in triggering those recollections; and our first apartment was the scene of at least a couple of those food-related reminiscences.

One occasion that comes to mind involved the preparation of a "gourmet" meal for a favorite aunt and uncle who had come in from New York for a family wedding. Being newly married, I was hoping to impress them with both my husband and my culinary skills. Well, in the end, success was mine on both counts, and while they loved my husband, the meal could really have gone either way. At about that time, we had adopted our first dog, Chester, a cocker spaniel/Labrador retriever/pig cross. Or so it seemed; that dog, the most lovable, irresistible animal imaginable, could truly have been part pig. He ate everything in sight including food-splattered cookbooks!

Well, I had only been counting on four for dinner—my aunt, uncle, husband, and myself—and not for a minute had I considered that Chester might be joining us for a fine meal of veal Marsala, pasta, and Caesar salad, followed by chocolate soufflé for dessert. Oh, what a fool I was to turn my back on that dog and my very, very expensive partially prepared, milk-fed veal scallopini.

As the recipe instructed, I had browned the meat and taken it out of the pan in order to prepare the Marsala sauce. I placed the platter with the veal on the kitchen table until I needed to return it to the pan. After starting the wine sauce, I made a quick dash into the living room to listen in on the conversation and refill glasses before heading back to finish preparations. As I entered the kitchen, my eyes were instantly drawn to Chester, lying flat out in the middle of the floor, luxuriously licking his lips. I swear to this day that he smiled at me in gratitude. There on the platter were a mere three medallions of veal, my beautiful meal virtually halved by this dog. What was I to do? How would I stretch the main course? How would I cover up the scarcity of the *pièce de résistance*? Or, should I just throw it all out since Chester had probably contaminated all of it? After my silent screams at Chester diminished, I decided that in this particular case, more was best—more mushrooms in the sauce, more pasta and salad on the plates. An "Oh, I'm not really feeling like having meat tonight," might work and a "Please, everybody, go right ahead; I'm actually full just from cooking the food!" could divert attention from my meatless plate. I know that I didn't fool anyone; the aroma of the veal poured forth from Chester's mouth, so it was pretty apparent that something had happened. On subsequent visits with my aunt and uncle, they would laughingly allude to the dinner for five that they had so enjoyed at our apartment.

While it was the veal Marsala that took centre stage that evening, the chocolate soufflé dessert carries its own set of fond and humorous memories as well. It was an absolute favorite of anyone who had the opportunity to try it, my mother-in-law included, or perhaps especially. Mary went so far as to ask for my recipe after she tasted it. I was thrilled and proud that she considered it so very good that she too wanted to bake it. I should have known better, of course. After she had made and tried it, she called me up for a recipe recap.

"Something's not quite right'" Mary told me. "Maybe I wrote it down incorrectly."

"Let's see," I said. "Here's the list of ingredients: confectioners' sugar, light cream, cream cheese, melted semisweet chocolate."

Mary hesitated and then informed me that, "You know, Janet, I ran out of confectioners' sugar and substituted fruit sugar. And about that light cream; I only had some Dream Whip in the fridge. Do you think that bittersweet chocolate would have made a difference?"

Well, it hadn't been the first time and certainly it wasn't the last time that my mother-in-law re-created one of my recipes, always with poetic license and with somewhat interesting results. But such a great dessert deserves to be baked as it really was intended!

# Chocolate Soufflé

## Ingredients

- ⅓ cup light cream
- 1 3-ounce package cream cheese
- ½ cup semisweet chocolate pieces
- 3 egg yolks
- Dash of salt
- 3 egg whites
- 3 tablespoons confectioners' sugar

## Preparation

Preheat the oven to 300°F.

Blend cream and cheese over very low heat. Add chocolate pieces and heat and stir until melted. Cool. Beat egg yolks and salt until thick and lemon-colored. Gradually blend into chocolate mixture. Beat egg whites until soft peaks form; gradually add sugar, beating to stiff peaks. Fold into chocolate mixture.

Pour into an ungreased 1-quart soufflé dish and bake in a slow (300°F.) oven for 45 minutes or until a knife inserted comes out clean. Delicious with vanilla ice cream.

Serves 5–6.

---

**Janet Caplan** lives with her husband, two spaniels, and an occasional daughter or two in Sooke, British Columbia, a wonderful maritime town on the west coast of Vancouver Island. In addition to writing, hiking, and reading books, Janet works part time as a bookkeeper.

# *Raspberries and Tea*

**Brianna Cedes**

At the counter of the high-end deli, we bought food for our first afternoon together. Henry appeared to be totally at ease. I was excited and nervous. We choose cheese, a baguette that we would later tear apart, chocolates, red wine, and raspberries in honey syrup. Looking at the raspberries, their dark red flesh curled into tiny succulent cups, I asked, "Do you like to put your tongue into the little hole?" Up shot his bushy eyebrows!

"Of course!" he grinned and his light blue eyes gleamed wickedly at me. So many of my memories of him involve food! He had no interest in health foods, nutritional content, or calories. Food was to be enjoyed, savored, relished, and shared. His approach to food was about sensuality and connection.

Henry filled my largest soup pot with piles of washed spinach leaves, and handfuls of raisins and pine nuts. After the spinach steamed down to soft, dark green leaves, he tossed in olive oil and sharp pepper. We ate it with grated cheese on slippery pasta. We ate lobster together, and mussels, licking the winey, garlicky broth from our fingers. He grilled huge, juicy hamburgers for my children and me, and served them on toasted English muffins, with ketchup, mayo, and "little pickle circles."

In the summer, we sometimes ate outside, at his uncle's home, in a beautiful garden of vegetables and wildflowers. Beyond the garden were grasses and scrubby trees; past the fence, the land sloped down toward the bay. Rabbits visited the garden, and Henry gave my children salt shakers and instructions to wait quietly for the bunnies. "If you can sprinkle some salt on the bunny's tail, then you can catch it," he solemnly told them. He made sun tea, setting out water and bags of tea in big cylindrical glass jars stoppered with thick, wide corks. One summer afternoon, he photographed my little dark-haired daughter smiling beside a jar of amber-colored tea. Henry baked chocolate cake and created ice cream concoctions for birthdays. In warm weather, he made thick chocolate malts; in the winter, pots of hot chocolate with marshmallows and cinnamon, his glasses fogging from the steam.

During the day as we worked together, we drank endless cups of Earl Grey tea, the strong flavor softened with sugar and milk. When I smell the bergamot aroma of that tea, I always think of him at the stove, brewing the tea correctly. The dark brown-red berries on the wallpaper that covered the walls and the ceiling in the kitchen were the exact color of the tea.

Our business went belly up. What followed was a year of fears that neither of us dared to share, misunderstandings, and too many conflicting demands. I found a job in another city, and the children and I moved away. After some years, when our anger and disappointment had cooled, we cautiously began writing. Every Monday morning, I would find an email message from him, often with a recipe or a description of a meal. He married. For a while, he and his wife Marta lived on a houseboat, and he wrote about making sun tea and grilling fish on the deck of the boat.

---

**Brianna Cedes** has recently begun writing, after twenty years of teaching science on the primary and secondary levels in public schools. Her favorite part of her work was encouraging young girls to think about having careers in the sciences. She has four grandchildren, and occasionally does messy science experiments in the kitchen with them.

# *Birthday Ice Cream with Raspberries*

### Ingredients

- 1 pint chocolate ice cream
- 1 pint vanilla ice cream
- 3 Heath bars
- 1 teaspoon instant espresso coffee
- 1 pint fresh raspberries

### Preparation

Line an 8x4-inch loaf pan with a generous amount of plastic wrap overflowing the sides. Let the pint of chocolate ice cream melt into liquid form. Pour it into the loaf pan and place in the freezer.

When the chocolate ice cream is frozen hard, let the vanilla ice cream melt. While the vanilla is melting, chop up the Heath bars into small dice. Mix with the teaspoon of instant espresso. Stir this into the melted vanilla ice cream. Pour the vanilla ice cream–Heath bars–instant espresso mixture over the frozen chocolate ice cream, wrap the plastic wrap over the top, and return it to the freezer.

Place the plate on which you will serve the ice cream dessert into the freezer for about 30 minutes before use. Immediately before serving, unwrap the frozen loaf of ice cream onto the chilled plate.

Use a hot knife to cut slices (alternatively, although not so attractively, use an ice cream scoop to serve). Serve with fresh raspberries to sprinkle over each portion.

Serves 6–8.

### Tips and Notes

You can vary this recipe all sorts of ways:

- Use M&Ms instead of diced Heath bar;
- Add ½ teaspoon of cinnamon or more to taste instead of instant espresso;
- Sprinkle with blueberries instead of raspberries.

---

He sent chocolates to my children and sent me kitchen gifts—aged balsamic vinegar, fragrant olive oil, a baker's knife. I sent him music and tee shirts with opera logos. In his last message, Henry wrote that a growth had been found in his intestines and asked me not to try to contact him.

About a year after Henry's death, I visited his daughter Beth and her family. The baby, eleven months old, had Henry's blue eyes and soft blonde hair. Seven-year-old Janey sat on my lap and read me a storybook. She showed me the necklace that she had made herself and worn to her grandfather's funeral. It was cold, and in the late afternoon, Beth brewed Earl Grey tea. She served it properly, from a pretty china teapot, with milk and sugar. The chatter and laughter of the four children pulled me back into the present, away from my memories. Then Beth reminded her daughters, "Do you remember? Grandpa always loved to drink this tea."

# Passover Requirements:
## Attendance at the Seder and Strawberry Schaum Torte

**Judith Helburn**

When I was a child, the family would go to Pappy's for special occasions. Pappy's, a barbecue rib and steak house, was owned by a friend of my parents. The best part of the experience was the dessert, a choice of meringue tortes with various fillings.

One special year, Mom teased the recipe for Strawberry *Schaum* Torte from their friend, and from that date onward, Strawberry *Schaum* Torte was the featured dessert on Passover, the Jewish holiday that celebrates freedom, the exodus of the Israelites from Egypt. There are many food restrictions during the eight days of Passover, the universal one being that we are not to use ordinary flour and leavening because the Israelites were in such a rush to escape from their existence of slavery that they did not have time for their bread to rise. Thus, for eight days, those who are observant eat dry, cardboard-like matzo instead of bread—to remember that *we* were once slaves in the land of Egypt.

We get around the leavening part by whipping up many egg whites. When my husband and I were married many, many years ago, I went through Mom's recipe box and copied about a dozen recipes. Naturally, Strawberry *Schaum* Torte was one of them. I have continued Mom's tradition for over forty-five years now. I find the promise of a small mountain of white meringue, soft in the middle and crisp on the outside, topped with whipped cream and strawberries with bright yellow lemon sauce dripping down the sides has kept first our children and then our grandchildren moving through the dinner ritual and service. "Slackers, of course, get no dessert."

There is absolutely no reason in the world not to make it any other time. But, in my house, it is served only once a year, at the first Passover Seder evening meal and reading of the story about when *we* were slaves in Egypt. Strawberry *Schaum* Torte is a sure way to bring wandering family members back home for Passover.

---

**Judith Helburn,** SCN Board Past President, feels that the most effective way to grow and bloom is to do life repair, face one's own mortality, and to give back. Developing one's spirituality is the backbone of what she teaches. She feels that many women, especially older women, feel as if they have led uninteresting lives in the shadow of others. No matter what one believes, telling one's story is the way to live on.

# *Strawberry Schaum Torte*

### Ingredients

| | |
|---|---|
| 8–10 | egg whites at room temperature |
| ⅛ | teaspoon salt |
| ⅛ | teaspoon cream of tartar |
| 2 | cups sugar |
| 1 | teaspoon vanilla |
| ½ | cup ground almonds (optional) |
| | Strawberries, no sugar |
| | Whipped cream, no sugar |

### Preparation

Preheat the oven to 300°F. Beat the egg whites until foamy, then add salt and cream of tartar and beat until stiff. Add sugar by the ¼ cup. Add vanilla and almonds. Pour into an ungreased 8-inch or 9-inch spring-form pan saving 1 cup of meringue to make "kisses." Place "kisses" of meringue on top, using a large spoon. Bake at 300°F. for 45–60 minutes, or until it doesn't look moist. If it starts browning, cover it with a paper bag. Cool in the pan in the oven.

Loosen the sides with a metal spatula and remove the spring-form pan. Pull the "kisses" of meringue off the top of the large meringue torte and set the kisses aside. **Do not refrigerate.** Spread a layer of whipped cream on the large meringue torte, then a layer of cut strawberries. Place the meringue kisses and some whole strawberries around the edge to decorate. Serve immediately.

Serves 8–10.

### Tips and Notes

You can also serve this with a lemon sauce made from the egg yolks.

# *Lemon Sauce*

### Ingredients

| | |
|---|---|
| 1 | tablespoon potato starch |
| ½ | cup sugar |
| ½ | cup water |
| 2 | small lemons, grated rinds and juice |
| 4 | beaten egg yolks |

### Preparation

Combine potato starch and sugar. Blend in water. Stir in lemon. Blend in yolks. Cook over low flame, stirring. Beat until cooked and glossy. Serve on the side.

### Tips and Notes

The Strawberry *Schaum* Torte is best assembled and decorated right before dinner or even after dinner.

If there are leftover's (doubtful) refrigerate, but the crisp part softens.

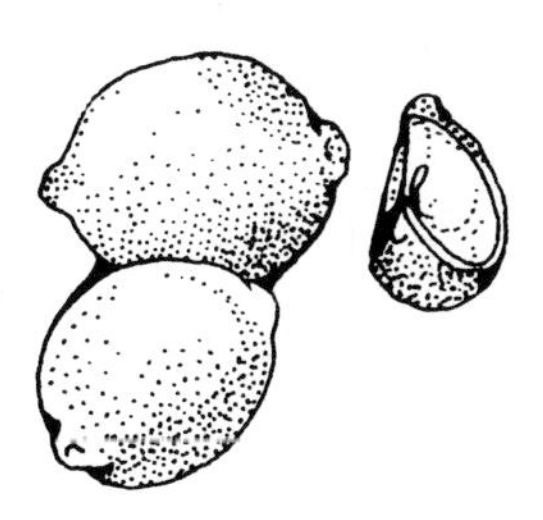

# *The Last Recipe*

**Jane Cadieux**

*Dear Jane,*

*I'm sending this recipe from Anita's computer. She's not well today. Call later to discuss.*

*Anita sends love and so do I.*

*Lise*

My mother-in-law Anita had just begun chemotherapy when she had asked Lise to send that email from her home, thousands of miles from mine. I knew the chemo was making Anita ill but we weren't worried. She'd recover by summer. Even in illness, she could not be distracted from an on-going long-distance discussion we were having about a chocolate pudding-cake, a discussion that had begun a few years back—long before she got sick—the day after my husband and I dined in a small expensive restaurant on the Swiss/French border. As I scanned the dessert menu that evening, I decided on something called a *moelleux*. When the gooey chocolate concoction arrived, I burst out laughing.

"What's the matter?" My husband was surprised.

"This dessert reminds me of a pudding-cake mix I loved as a child.

"Yes, I remember! I loved that cake." A smile spread across his face as he reminisced about his childhood summers at his lakeside cabin with no electricity and an ancient gas oven.

"That cake never failed. Was it Betty Crocker or Duncan Hines?" he pondered.

"Your mother would know," I told him. "I'll call her tomorrow."

We both continued to giggle over the elegant dessert that had awakened memories of its packaged predecessor from forty years earlier. But, I had just learned something new about my mother-in-law, the woman whose cooking rivaled the world's top chefs, who had even met some of them in a long diplomatic career, whose culinary passion began in childhood around a dining room table of thirteen brothers and sisters, whose ease in the kitchen was not just to cook food but to live it. Until that evening, I never knew my mother-in-law made anything out of a box.

When I first met Anita, I was a college student with cooking skills that didn't extend beyond the preparation of a macaroni dinner. I was dating her son and she, seeing at once his interest in me, wasted no time immersing me into her world. I was invited to an informal dinner at the house. When I stepped through the door, she immediately put me to work chopping the vegetables for a *macédoine de légumes*. Her husband and younger son polished the crystal and set the table while my new boyfriend, the elder son, cranked an antiquated ice-cream machine. An informal dinner: I don't think so! I was nervous and shaky. It was bad enough meeting his parents for the first time, but I had never chopped anything, much less into neat, even cubes. I not only worried about adding a fingertip to the vegetable medley but anticipated the dreaded comment, "You're not doing it right!" It didn't come. Instead, Anita

---

**Jane Cadieux** started out in the business world as a fashion designer/merchandiser. But after one marriage, two children, three international moves and living life for the past thirteen years overseas, she has evolved into a wife, mother, teacher, volunteer, photographer, artist, writer...observer.

patiently showed me the correct way and soon I was happily chopping not realizing that I had just passed an important test—blending in to this sacred family activity. Chopping done, I sat and watched in awe as Anita whipped through each subsequent preparation from slicing potatoes with her mandolin to deglazing the roasting pan with *glace de viande* or "cook's gold," as she called it.

Her kitchen provided visual testimony to the depth of her passion. Counters exploded with gadgets, some resembling medieval torture devices, and she had a library devoted just to cookbooks, including the complete collection of *Gourmet* since 1941. Decades of pages torn from the newspapers were stuffed into files. Recipes hung on cupboard doors, burst out of books, lay scrawled on unopened mail. I knew what I had to do to win my way into her heart. Over the years, her influence transcended that of mentor–chef and mother-in-law. No subject was too tender to escape discussion while together we sautéed, fried, reduced, and simmered, our relationship mellowing into a deep friendship. If not the most brilliant student, I was, at least, an attentive one. I soaked up everything she said like a piece of bread soaking up a good sauce. Along with lessons on how to put the "hat" on the soufflé, or how to fix a curdled cream sauce, she was there for me—for my brightest days and darkest hours. And, that simple dessert, plucked from her archive of thousands? It was not the first recipe Anita sent me during our three-year pudding-cake discussion though according to her it was the best. It was also the last. I was glad to be there, in the end, for her—feeding her the last drops of food she would ever taste.

Her voice often comes back to me—answering my question in her sharp wit and French lilt, making me giggle as I did that night I dined on the *moelleux*... "It was made by Monarch. But rest assured, Jane, this 'from scratch' version is every bit as good as the one from the box."

# Hot Fudge Pudding Cake

### Ingredients

- 6 tablespoons unsalted butter
- 4 ounces best-quality bittersweet chocolate, chopped
- 1 cup all-purpose flour
- ¾ teaspoon double-acting baking powder
- ¾ teaspoon salt
- ⅔ cup unsweetened cocoa powder
- 2 large eggs
- 1 cup granulated sugar
- ½ cup milk
- 1 teaspoon vanilla
- ½ cup firmly packed light-brown sugar
- 1⅓ cups boiling water

### Preparation

Preheat oven to 350°F.

In a pan over very low heat, melt together butter and chocolate. Let cool. Sift together flour, baking powder, salt, and half the cocoa powder. In a large bowl, whisk together egg, sugar, milk, vanilla, and butter–chocolate mixture. Add the sifted dry ingredients. Stir batter until just combined.

Spread the batter evenly in an ungreased 8-inch square baking pan. In a small bowl, whisk together the remaining cocoa powder, brown sugar, and boiling water. Pour the mixture over the cake batter and bake the cake in the middle of the oven at 350°F. for 30–35 minutes or until a cake tester comes out slightly moist. Serve warm with ice cream.

Makes one 8-inch cake.

# *Starting Points – November, Fourth Week*

**A Writing Prompt**

*"Never eat more than you can lift."*
Miss Piggy

*"Food is the most primitive form of comfort."*
Sheila Graham

*"I've been on a diet for two weeks and all I've lost is two weeks."*
Totie Fields

As the holidays approach, many of us are thinking about food. This week, let's do some writing about it. Here are several questions to get you started.

- What are your favorite foods? Why? What do they mean to you?
- What are your least favorite foods? Why? Is there some secret symbolism here?
- Does your family have some holiday food traditions? What are they? Where did they come from?
- What's your family's favorite recipe? What's the story behind it?
- Many of us have "food issues." What are yours?
- If you don't have any "food issues," why not?

*This writing prompt is reprinted from* Starting Points: Weekly Writing Prompts for Women with Stories to Tell *by Susan Wittig Albert, founder of Story Circle Network. Used with permission of the author.* Starting Points *can be purchased through the Story Circle Network website.*

*To learn more about Story Circle Network, to purchase books, and to join our organization, visit the website:*

**www.storycircle.org**

# Index of Contributing Authors & Writing Prompts



**Writing Prompts**

# Index of Recipes